# The Church-Friendly Family

### Randy Booth
### &
### Rich Lusk

**Edited by Uri Brito**

**Foreword by John Barach**

**Covenant Media Press**
Nacogdoches, TX 75961

Randy Booth and Rich Lusk, *The Church-Friendly Family*

Edited by Uri Brito
Cover design by Anna Wedgeworth

**Published by Covenant Media Press**
8784 FM 226, Nacogdoches, TX 75961
www.CMFnow.com

Printed in the United States of America.

ISBN: 978-1- 62407-305-2

# Dedication

To Mickey Schneider,
faithful laborer,
masterful story-teller,
shepherd of the flock,
mentor,
and friend.
May the Church continue to benefit
from your passion and loyalty
to the gospel proclamation.

# Contents

# Authors

**Randy Booth** pastors Grace Covenant Presbyterian Church in Nacogdoches, TX. Pastor Booth has been married to his wife Marinell for 38 years and they have three grown children and twelve grandchildren. He has overseen the planting and establishment of six churches, is the director of Covenant Media Foundation, a conference speaker, co-founder of Veritas Classical Christian School in Texarkana, AR, and served as the chairman of the founding board of Regents Academy in Nacogdoches, TX, where he is currently the chaplain. Hh is member of the Board of Trustees of New ST. Andrews College, and is the author of numerous published articles and books, including, *Children of the Promise, To You and Your Children, The Case for Covenantal Infant Baptism,* and *The Standard Bearer.*

**Rich Lusk** pastors Trinity Presbytery Church in Birmingham, AL. Prior to that, he was on staff at Auburn Avenue Presbyterian Church in Monroe, LA, and Redeemer Presbyterian Church in Austin, TX. Rich has written numerous internet and journal articles, contributed to several books, and authored *Paedofaith.* Rich holds a B.S. from Auburn University and a M. A. from the University of Texas. He is married to Jenny and together they have four children.

# Acknowledgments

These lectures were delivered at the nineteenth Family Advance Conference in Sandestin, Florida. Over the years, the conference has stressed a variety of topics ranging from cultural to family issues. In 2009, the conference brought two speakers—Randy Booth and Rich Lusk—to discuss the role of the Church in the life of the family and society. Pastors, parents, and parishioners will benefit from these seven lectures.

I had the privilege of introducing these speakers, delivering a lecture entitled "The Future of the Family," and moderating the question and answer period. At the end of the conference, Rev. Mickey Schneider, moved by the substance contained in these lectures, encouraged me to put them into a readable format in the hope that they would serve the broader Reformed and Evangelical community. The process took longer than I had expected and would have bogged down, until I sought the aid of Pastor John Barach. This book would not be available now were it not for his insights and invaluable contributions. To him I am deeply grateful.

I also wish to express my gratitude to Pastors Al Stout and Rob Hadding. Our lengthy conversations over the years on the glories of Church have increased my joy in serving and shepherding the saints.

My lovely wife Melinda has provided constant encouragement, even when at times I doubted this labor would see the light of day. Obrigada, meu amor!

I am also profoundly grateful for the grammatical genius of Ron Gilley and Matt Bianco who have offered their time to carefully read through the manuscript and propose salient advice, thus improving the readability of this work.

My special thanks to Mickey Schneider, who is now approaching the end of his pastoral duties at Trinity Presbyterian Church in Valparaiso, Florida. He has been a faithful mentor to me and continues to provide pastoral wisdom.

I suppose it is now befitting to assume responsibility for any mistakes. I do so fearfully, but with the knowledge that I have faithful friends and family who will console and cheer me on in future endeavors. May our Triune God be praised, and may the gates of hell fear the labors of Jesus' Bride.

                                        Uri Brito

# Foreword

*John Barach*

It doesn't take much insight to figure out that the family is in trouble these days. Whether you think about single moms and deadbeat dads, about domineering husbands or lazy couch potatoes, about rebellious children and their apparently helpless parents, about same-sex marriage and rampant no-fault divorce, about sibling rivalry and all the other dysfunctions to which marriages and families are prone, all of these things support the case that marriage and family are in a mess. Sure, you know couples with solid marriages and families with well-behaved, happy, fat-souled children, but they aren't the norm, are they? The way they stand out only makes it clarifies how bad the situation is.

The family is in trouble, but if we look at Scripture, we see that the family has been in trouble from the beginning. Adam betrayed his brand-new bride, standing by "with her" (Gen. 3:8) and allowing her to be deceived by the serpent. Cain murdered his brother and then founded a city, characterized eventually by polygamy and murderous vengeance—and the sons of God saw the beauty of the daughters of that city, the daughters of men, and married them, corrupting the line of the godly. From then on, Scripture presents families scarred by betrayal, favoritism, conflict, murder, sexual sin, intermarriage with the ungodly, and more.

The family is in trouble, and the good news is that the family can be restored in Christ. Salvation is not individualistic. Jesus did not die simply so that certain individuals could be forgiven and restored to new life. He died so that relationships could be restored, so that every aspect of life, including our families, might be healed and made new.

But how can that healing take place? If it is obvious that the family is in trouble today, it is equally obvious that a great number of people are aware of that trouble and want help—and there is plenty of help being offered in books and essays and lectures and radio programs and blog entries and Facebook statuses. But many times that help, valuable as it can be, is still missing something. It's missing the right context.

In this collection of essays, Randy Booth and Rich Lusk—two pastors and family men—remind us that healing for our families is found in right relationship to God through Jesus Christ and that the context for that healing is the Church, which is the body of Christ.

Our families are not ultimate, and they will not be restored and glorified by an exclusive focus on the family. In fact, if we make our family and its well-being our highest priority, we sow the seeds of our family's destruction. Rather, our families must be placed in the context of the family of God. The nuclear family does not simply need more advice or exhortation; it needs Jesus and it needs His body.

Only if we make our families "Church-friendly"—only by putting our families in the context of the Church, by putting Christ and His people first, by bringing our families to share in the Church's worship, fellowship, calling, and mission—will our families be restored, and more than that, be transformed from glory to glory.

# Editor's Introduction

The title *The Church-Friendly Family* is quite purposeful. The authors wish to emphasize a particular vision for families, a vision grounded in a biblical sociology. In fact, it is an old vision declared throughout the Church and the Reformation, which needs to be reasserted. The vision is to call fathers and mothers to exercise their parental duties within an ecclesiastical paradigm.

By God's grace, we have seen a joyful shift over the years in many of our churches. We have rightly reconsidered program-saturated churches and found them wanting. Though not intentionally, these churches have dismantled the family by separating family members. Worship—which is fundamental to familial maturity—has been dispensed in crumbs and what is eaten is largely unsatisfying.

The Psalms—Yahweh's inspired song book—are filled with the language of death. There is agony and uncertainty throughout many of Israel's songs (Psalms 6, 32, 38, 51, 102, 130, 143). But these same psalms conclude on a different note: one of relief, renewed trust, and rest. The uncertainty was only the first step in the long journey from infancy to maturity.

## The Future of the Family

The psalms symbolize the triumph of God the Father through the death and resurrection of the Son. There is inherent in psalmic theology a death/resurrection theme. In fact, this theme is fundamental to understanding redemptive history. History tells us of the death of old empires. These empires died so that a new and indestructible empire might arise. Evil kings died so that a new and righteous King might arise. The old man died to make room for a new man. The old Adam must die, so a new Adam could rise and bring healing to the nations. Through the final Adam, the nations will come and feast; through His resurrection, the great congregation and brotherhood of saints will sing the praises of Yahweh.

It is my contention that the biological family will taste of the glorious future only after it dies and is raised anew. The natural family needs to be torn apart and divided by God's two-edged sword. The family needs to live the messianic life of abandonment, so that it may live the messianic life of glory. This is what Jesus means when he says: "Whoever finds his life will lose it, and whoever loses his life for my sake will find it" (Matt 10:39). The family must undergo a theology of the cross before it can experience the theology of glory.

## Biblical Priorities: Death and Change

Death was the consequence of Adam's autonomous decision in the garden. Death is the end result of rebellion. Our biblical priorities will determine whether or not we wish to follow Adam's path. The family also is faced with a similar question if it wishes to grow into wisdom. If we truly believe in maturation into biblical priorities, then we must be prepared to reconsider the future of the family. Is it following the Adamic pattern or is it forming for itself a new pattern of thinking?

## The Family and the Church

The sixteenth-century Reformation began to restore marriage in the home. Years of religious and cultural immorality began to see a new day through Martin Luther. The German Reformer once wrote: "I urge matrimony on others with so many arguments that I am myself almost moved to marry."[1] Shortly after, Luther married Katherine von Bora. Centuries of negative writings on women were reversed, or better, reformed through Luther's marriage. One scholar explains how Luther lived his life: "Luther's faith was simple enough to trust that after a conscientious day's labor, a Christian father could come home and eat his sausage, drink his beer, play his flute, sing with his children, and make love to his wife—all to the glory of God!"[2]

The Reformation reformed the individual family. It gave it a new identity. But the Reformation also maintained its biblical priorities. It restored the family, but it did not exalt the family above all institutions. It would have been easy to do so, since the Church was deeply corrupt. The Reformers could have said, "Let's end the institutional Church and place the individual family as supreme," but this is not what the Reformers did. The reason the Reformation did not exalt the biological family was because the Reformation knew that only one family held God's ultimate

---

[1] Martin Luther, *Luther's Correspondence and Other Contemporary Letters*, trans. and ed. Preserved Smith and Charles M. Jacobs, 2 vols. (Philadelphia: Lutheran Publication Society, 1918), 2:304.

[2] William Lazareth, *Luther on the Christian Home: An Application of the Social Ethics of the Reformation* (Philadelphia: Muhlenberg, 1960), 145.

affection. The Reformation knew that only the Jerusalem above—the eternal family—which will never perish and which is our true mother. As Cyprian wrote—and John Calvin echoed— "You cannot have God as father unless you have the Church as mother." Paul affirms this in Galatians 4 and the Westminster Confession affirms this when it says that outside the church, "the kingdom of the Lord Jesus Christ, the house and family of God, . . . there is no ordinary possibility of salvation" (25.2). Calvin viewed the work of the Church, the work of exercising the keys to the kingdom, as the supreme act of God in this world. The Church was to Calvin a sacred institution that was dearest to the heart of God. As Gary North once wrote: "History moves from the *Adamic family of man* in the garden of Eden toward the *adopted family of God* in the city of God, the New Jerusalem (Rev. 21; 22)."[3]

The biological family begins to embrace this eschatological view of the Scriptures when it embraces the narrative of the Church of Christ as God's true, central, and eternal family.

## The Church as God's Weapon

The Church is God's greatest masterpiece. It is not a man-made institution; it is the creation of God the Father, Son, and Spirit. It is the fiery weapon that God uses to pierce the hearts of men. The Church is made new by the Pentecostal fire of Acts 2. She is the undoing of Babel. Whereas in Babel God separated the families of the earth, in the Church Christ brings the nations of the earth together to form one holy and undivided family. Mark Horne

---

[3] Gary North, *Baptized Patriarchalism: The Cult of the Family* (Tyler, TX: Institute for Christian Economics, 1995), 30.

observes that in the Church, "men and women are called upon to be separated from their natural identities as members of race and class and be given a new Spiritual identity by being added to the body of Christ in baptism."[4] The inescapable conclusion is that if you are united to Christ, you must be united to Christ's Church. The Spirit that creates new life in the believer is the Spirit that unites the people to Christ's bride.

Our modern culture has been taught to trivialize the Church and to treat her as a second-class citizen in the kingdom of God. We generally agree that the Church is important, but an answer filled with skepticism arises when we ask, "Is it essential for the well-being of Christ's kingdom?" We must affirm the supremacy of the Church among all the spheres and institutions of human life by placing ourselves within the life and mission of the Church. This is not an easy step, but it is a necessary step, a step that crucifies the old way of thinking.

## Who Controls the World Controls the Future

In the world, whoever has the primacy over all spheres rules the world. Christ very clearly placed the Church as the primary keeper of the mysteries and wisdom of the gospel. Paul cherishes this idea so much that in Ephesians he writes that, "through the church the manifold wisdom of God might now be made known to the rulers and authorities in the heavenly places" (Eph. 3:10). What is most important in the eyes of God will control the future and will affect everything around it. The failures of the state

---

[4] Mark Horne, "A Body Formed by the Spirit: A Sermon on the Church," online: http://www.hornes.org/theologia/mark-horne/sermon-a-body-formed-by-the-spirit.

and family are a result of the failures of the Church to properly accomplish her mission. The Church's primacy over all earthly institutions teaches the family unit to look to the Church as God's primary headquarters, since the Church is the true family of God.

God adopts individuals from every tongue, nation, and people. He adopts orphans and widows into a family where there are no orphans and widows. In the family of God, widows find a faithful husband in Christ and brothers and sisters can never be separated because they are adopted into an inseparable family. In the Church, there is no incomplete family. In God's family, there is no divorce, because Christ is eternally bound to his bride.

It is a legitimate endeavor, and one that God honors, when we strengthen our own families with family worship, with love, and with deep relationships with one another, but in the words of Gary North, "Any attempt to strengthen the family without also strengthening the institutional Church is self-defeating for Christians."[5] We need to consider our actions within our individual families in terms of how they will strengthen the Church of Christ. Should we give our children an explicitly Christian education? Unquestionably. Do we do it only because we will produce better theologians and better citizens of the state? No. We do it because it will produce better worshippers of Yahweh in the Church. Should we have family worship regularly in our homes? Unquestionably. Do we do it only because it unites us as family members? No. We do it because it will produce better worshipers in God's gathered assembly. This is the outlook we need to adopt if we are to think biblically about the future and conform ourselves to the counsel of God.

---

[5] North, *Baptized Patriarchalism*, 2.

The Church is the center of God's world. The Church—as possessor of truth and possessor of the mysteries of God—demonstrates to the world that unless they join her they will perish. The mission of the Church is the heart of God's mission for the world. And since the future of the natural family is not based on the centrality of the natural family but on the centrality of God's new cosmic and supernatural family, then the future of the individual family is a future found in the Church. The family must die so that it may be raised to a new status, so that it may embrace the glorious and eternal family of the Church. But how can this changing of priorities take place? Is this simply theological nitpicking? On the contrary, I believe it has serious consequences for the way individual families think and live.

First, because the Church is at the center of God's affections does not mean that God does not love the family. The family is important in God's plan of redeeming the world; however, the family fulfills its role when it conscientiously aligns itself with the mission of the Church. For the family to isolate itself from the Church is self-destructive. It must join God's new creation-family: the family which was birthed by the Spirit.

Second, we need to abandon any individualistic tendencies we may have. We are a corporate body; we are given gifts, as St. Paul says, "to care for one another" (I Corinthians 12:25). This implies a rich understanding of fellowship and community. We must embrace this ecclesiastical culture in full. We are called to embrace this new society, to embrace its culture and rituals, learning to feast and to build one another up in strength and holiness.

xx            *Editor's Introduction*

Third, changing our priorities means living the life of accountability within the Church. It means living in light of Matthew 18, and in light of the potential for apostasy and discipline. If a father has trained his family to think that discipline happens only within the family, he has failed in his job. But if a father teaches his family that he is accountable to his elders and pastor, then the family realizes that even the father is not above the law. There is a greater punishment than being punished by the family; it is the punishment of excommunication. The Church's authority to excommunicate is the most fearful sanction in history.

Finally, the nuclear family is the instrument God has established to support his greatest joy: the Church. Thus, the family incorporated into the Church serves for the sake of the world. It is involved in the process of bringing in other families to join in the great cosmic family of God. The family needs to be re-born into the New Jerusalem above. It needs to assume its responsibility as part of a New Creation-body. It must be crucified, so it can be raised into a new perspective on life. The family comes to the Lord's Day liturgical celebration to die and to be raised into God's new adopted family. The family loses its identity in the congregation of the righteous and takes on a new identity. Peter Leithart describes the transformation that occurs when God's people gather for corporate worship:

> Many of you came here as families, but during this hour the borders of your family dissolve and you come before the Lord as a single family. That liturgical dissolution of the family is not permanent. It is a moment of renewal. Like all deaths, the ritual death of your individual family in the liturgy is a

step toward resurrection. After you have gathered here as the single household of faith, gathered at this one table, you disperse to your separate homes and tables, renewed by assembly in God's house, by God's Word, by God's food.[6]

After dying, being raised, and then incorporated into this glorious family, we can see the future of God's kingdom through new eyes; the eyes of a united Church, a Church established for God's glory, which shall never perish. May these essays embolden us for the work of the Church, and may our families join and delight in her mission.

Uri Brito
Pentecost Season, 2012

---

[6] Peter J. Leithart, "Eucharistic Exhortation, Fourth Sunday of Lent," online: http://www.leithart.com/archives/002874.php.

# Chapter 1
# Family and Culture
*Randy Booth*

## Creation

When God created man in knowledge, righteousness, and holiness, with dominion over the creatures, and told him to be fruitful and multiply, that was a mandate to fill the earth with *godly* people who would produce a *godly culture.* That is what godly people do. The goal was not to multiply misery or to populate hell but rather to advance God and His kingdom. The introduction of sin fouled the planet. In fact, it made it green: green with envy. Sin corrupted the culture. Soon thereafter, God promised a Redeemer.

This redemptive work unfolded throughout the Old Testament. The Old Testament closes in Malachi with reminders that God, among other things, wants husbands to be devoted to their wives, families to produce godly children, and the hearts of fathers and children to be turned toward one another. This, the Lord said, would prevent the land from being smitten with a curse.

The New Testament then opens with John the Baptist—whom Jesus identifies as Elijah—preparing the way for the Savior who would accomplish all of this through the gospel. However, the first work of the gospel is a work of separation:

Do not think that I came to bring peace on earth. I did not come to bring peace but a sword. For I have come to "set a man against his father, a daughter against her mother, and a daughter-in-law against her mother-in-law"; and "a man's enemies will be those of his own household." He who loves father or mother more than Me is not worthy of Me. And he who loves son or daughter more than Me is not worthy of Me. And he who does not take his cross and follow after Me is not worthy of Me (Matt. 10:34–38).

On the face of it this does not sound like a very "family-friendly" program. If there is to be redemption—if there is to be a recovery from the fall—then a radical break from the fallen way of doing things must occur. So, the Savior lays His claim on us first, and then He calls us to walk away from everyone and everything in order to follow Him. He even initially separates us from our family so that new families can emerge. These are redeemed families who will now fill the earth with a new humanity, with godly children. What Jesus does after we forsake everything is send us back as new men—husbands, wives, and parents—and send us back to material things to use for His glory. The Church—the Body of Christ—is the starting place of our redemption. From there we are sent out to represent and serve Him. The Church is an outpost of the kingdom of God. From *there* we are sent back to our families *to establish outposts of the Church.* And thus, we need families that are oriented first and foremost toward Christ and His Body—the Church. We need Church-friendly families. Then and only then can we expect to see our families truly transformed:

transformed men and women, transformed families, and ultimately a transformed world.

Sin is the destroyer of lives. Thus, people come to the Church in all kinds of conditions and with all kinds of baggage. The Church begins by accepting people the way they are. But the work of the Church does not stop with acceptance because the work of redemption is about changing people. They cannot stay the way they are. All things have become new!

For the purposes of introducing the topic of "Family and Culture," it is important for us to see the *primacy of the Church* over ourselves and our families. When our priorities are straight—that is, when Jesus is indeed Lord—then His followers will see a transformation. A family culture will emerge that will truly be salt and light in a rotting and dark world.

## Charting a Course

Do you like the culture you see? If so, then we should keep doing what we're doing. If not, then we have to chart a new course. If you follow the trajectory of the broader culture, where do your children and grandchildren land? Scripture tells us that we are to think in terms of our children and our children's children and, therefore, to act in faithfulness to God and His Word. In fact, the sons of Issachar are commended in the Bible for understanding the times in which they lived and for knowing what Israel ought to do (1 Chr. 12:23). Do we really understand our times, and do we know what to do in the Church and in our families? Where are the deficits in the broader culture and are those deficiencies being self-consciously addressed in your home? For starters, I would suggest that the broader culture clearly lacks leadership, respect, and love, and thus our homes—the outposts of the Church—should be pictures of leadership, respect, and love. We tend to think of culture as something that is "out there" and as having an influence on us and our families. But a culture is found anywhere there is a community of people. It is through culture that our way of living is transmitted from one generation to the next.

As Henry Van Til put it, "Culture is religion externalized." This is another way of saying that our ideas or beliefs have consequences and that these consequences are visible in our communities. We might consider this the "practical" side of philosophy. It matters what we think. Every idea produces a particular kind of fruit. Every culture is the product of ideas. For example, President Obama is the product of years of ideas generated by "Liberation Theology" taught to him by Rev. Jeremiah Wright. He now hopes to lead us all in a similar direction. That's what leaders do.

However, not only do ideas have consequences but consequences have ideas. In other words, we can look at this from the other side. When we see a culture and its fruit (which is what we often see first), we must ask: "What ideas produced this culture? What is the theology behind what we are seeing?" Many times the ideas have not been thought about in a systematic way. We either don't evaluate the culture at all (it just is), or the ideas seem to be random and unconnected. You see, we all do philosophy, but we don't all do philosophy well. Our philosophies are frequently haphazard and inconsistent. As a result, the fruit of our philosophy is also haphazard and inconsistent. Since we are inevitably philosophers (i.e., we have ideas), we must strive to be consistently Christian in our philosophy.

## A Family Has a Culture

You are the Church, and you constantly represent the Church. With this in mind, we must remember that a family is a community, and thus, it too has a culture. Just as the broader culture influences family culture, so too family culture influences the other cultures with which it comes into contact. The family culture is a reflection of its ideas and beliefs. Some people are better than their beliefs and others are worse than their beliefs. What we say and what we do are often in conflict. What we do, however, is the ultimate reflection of what we believe. Thus, we can look at the culture of a family and get a picture of what that family's beliefs and values really are (Matt. 7:20). Paul writes, "For the weapons of our warfare are not carnal but mighty in God for pulling down strongholds, casting down arguments and every high thing that exalts itself against the knowledge of God, bringing every thought into captivity to the obedience of Christ" (2 Cor. 10:4–5). It is therefore essential that we develop self-conscious and distinctively Christian ideas about the family culture. What do we want the broader culture to look like? Then, we should set out to make our families a picture of that broader Christian culture.

## Cleaning Out the Garage

Our own views of a subject are often shaped by a variety of sources—family, friends, media, school, pop culture, church, the Bible, and so forth. We can't easily sort through all these influences and separate them because they are frequently jumbled together. In fact, they are likely blurred in our own minds, creating vague or fuzzy images. Therefore, if we are to learn to think more biblically, we must begin a winnowing process by which we evaluate our ideas in light of a sound theology, replacing old ideas with new ones.

Inevitably, we will find that we have to adjust our views, casting off many erroneous notions and adopting new and sometimes radical views in their place. Unfortunately, it is not uncommon for us to make minor adjustments and yet perceive them as major. We have often gone one mile in the right direction when, in fact, we need to go a hundred miles.

God created man in knowledge, righteousness, and holiness, with dominion over the creatures. By his rebellion, man forfeited his ability to do this well; a perverted man was the result. All kinds of difficulty and misery ensued, with conflicts in the family culture and the broader culture continuing and expanding. In the midst of this chaos, God sent His Son, the firstborn of a new humanity, the second Adam. This new man, who also had knowledge, righteousness, and holiness, with dominion over the creatures, is the Redeemer of fallen man. He is the model or image of what we are called to be.

Our transformation is our restoration to true humanity, and that true humanity doesn't look like the popular images of humanity. In fact, it is likely contrary to much of what we have picked up along the way. Cleaning out the garage is a dreaded task for most of us. There is a lot of junk we have collected over the years, and much of it needs to go. But if we want to build something useful we will need some space, some tools, and some plans. And what we need to build is a family culture that we can leave to our children and our children's children. We need to build a culture that is going to change the world!

## The Importance of an Image

I enjoy woodworking and, especially, furniture building. After cleaning out my garage, I always start with a set of plans. I need an image of what the project is going to look like when it is finished. Many times those plans look complicated. The project will usually require me to acquire new tools and develop new woodworking skills (e.g., how to curve wood). I sometimes doubt whether I can actually pull it off, and I certainly make mistakes along the way. It's almost always harder than I imagined it would be. But in the end—when the project is finished—I have created an heirloom, something that will be passed on for generations. We all have images in our heads of the way things are supposed to be, and over time, we become those images. This is why we have to be careful about what goes in, because what goes in eventually comes out.

Our mental images are partly and subtly formed from past experiences, including our own upbringing and the culture around us. Taking off the old man (old images) and putting on the new man (new images) is essential to our ceasing to be an old man and becoming a new man in Christ (Eph. 4:17). New images can and must be formed by the Word of God. Thus, we are not conformed to the world, but are transformed by the renewing of our minds (Rom. 12:2). For us, as the new humanity in Jesus Christ, everything has become new. Indeed, we are being conformed "to the image of His Son" (Rom. 8:29). The old images are replaced by new images, and thus, a new family culture emerges. It is essential that we have before our mind's eye the picture of God's ideals: an ideal father, husband, wife, mother, children, and household. These images will be grand—too grand at first. We all fall short of the glory of

God. But it is His redemptive work, the work of the Spirit in sanctification, that moves us in the direction of those new images. We will need to refer to them repeatedly.

Within the context of the broader evangelical Church we can hear men honestly attempting to speak to a corrupt culture and calling people to repent, but there is frequently no solid biblical culture to replace it with. Our churches are too often not filled with models of what a godly family culture looks like; for that we will first need some godly husbands and fathers to self-consciously form that image, and then lead their wives and children to catch the vision of a family culture that honors our calling in Christ.

## Following the Instructions

Back to my furniture-building: when the project looks complicated or overwhelming, I try to focus on a single piece. I can build that; I can follow those instructions. I can produce that one shape or element that is a part of the whole. I still need to see and remember the big picture. In fact, if I am ever to see the project come to completion, I will need to refer to the plans often, while focusing on the particular task before me. I read the directions, in their proper order, over and over again. I read them until I understand them. God's Word contains the plans and the directions for building a family culture. It is the Church's task to maintain and instruct her members in God's Word and to send her members out the door to their various outposts, where they self-consciously apply those lessons day-by-day. Indeed, it is a grand project, with challenges, frustrations, and failures, but also with much help and hope. The inspired Scriptures are for doctrine, reproof, correction, and instruction "that the man of God may be complete, thoroughly equipped for every good work" (2 Tim. 3:16–17).

We all begin this project of building a family culture with different skill-sets, experiences, tools, raw materials, and so on. Some aspects of the task will be easier than others. Some families will excel where others struggle. God knew this when He called us to the project. By His grace He is able to supply all of our needs in Christ. He does this by placing us in His Church to work alongside others. So, regardless of where we are when we begin, we must begin looking to Him who has begun a good work in us. In fact, the apostle Paul tells us that "we are His workmanship, created in Christ Jesus for good works, which God prepared beforehand that we should walk in them" (Eph. 2:10). A big part of those good works includes (for most of us), the building of a family culture that conforms to His plans.

## Step Back

As we individually come to Christ, He tells us that

> If anyone comes to Me and does not hate his father and mother, wife and children, brothers and sisters, yes, and his own life also, he cannot be My disciple. And whoever does not bear his cross and come after Me cannot be My disciple. . . . So likewise, whoever of you does not forsake all that he has cannot be My disciple (Luke 14:26–27, 33).

Following Jesus begins with forsaking our relationships with other people, ourselves, and our possessions. All of these relationships are corrupted by sin. As soon as we come to Him, He sends us back to all those relationships, to ourselves, and even to all our material possessions to truly love them as new men in Christ. We now go back to our wives and husbands and children and begin (by the grace of God) to rebuild a city, a community of grace. The streets need to be swept, some demolition must occur, and the ruins must be repaired.

If individuals are really transformed by the grace of God, it is inevitable that the cultures they live in will also be transformed. Thereby, the kingdom of God advances in the earth and the transformed family cultures—these individual outposts of the Body of Christ—change the world.

Step back and look at your own family culture; get an aerial view. The good and the bad, the beautiful and the ugly all have a trajectory; they all produce some kind of culture. So if you see parts of your family culture that do not look right—parts that are not reflecting the images of the heavenly Father, or of Christ and His Church—then stop doing what you are doing and replace them with something better. Remember, ideas have consequences. You need some new (old) ideas in order to improve on your family culture in order to reflect the Father and Jesus Christ to the world.

This is why sound biblical views of the Triune God (theology) are critical. We must know the persons and works of God well (doctrine/ideas) since these form the images to which we will conform.

Shallow or fuzzy images won't do. The Bible brings focus to the comprehensive vision of God's redemptive work, and that work extends as far as the curse is found. When God works in us, He also works through us to produce a godly culture that is transmitted to others and to the next generation. We become the salt and light of the world!

## Christ and His Church

God uses several images to describe the Church, which provide models for our marriages (Eph. 5:22–33), the parent-child relationship (Gal. 3:26), and the whole household (1 Tim. 3:15). Just as the Body of Christ—the Church—is a community of persons with diverse functions that inevitably produce a culture (1 Cor. 12:12–14), so too is the nuclear family, which is an outpost or extension of the Church. As we develop a stronger awareness of how the Church models these familial relationships, we will see the fruit of that instruction in our individual homes.

The Body of Christ is not a slice of the pie; it is the pie, and the family is a slice of that pie. Even within our daily family routines, we are never separated from Christ. Our cooking, eating, and drinking; our conversations, labors, and love-making; our finances, childrearing, discipline, and singing; our resting, playing, and hospitality; our praying, reading Scripture, and worshiping are all to be manifestations of the culture of Christ. Not one square inch is to be void of Him. Thus, it is in this daily context that we take the lessons—the theology, doctrine, and exhortations—of the Church back to our homes where we actually apply what we have learned. Do you discuss the sermons with your family?

There should be a self-conscious oozing out of love for God, and instruction from the Word of God, omnipresent in our families:

> Hear, O Israel: The LORD our God, the LORD is one! You shall love the LORD your God with all your heart, with all your soul, and with all your strength. And these words which I command you

today shall be in your heart. You shall teach them diligently to your children, and shall talk of them when you sit in your house, when you walk by the way, when you lie down, and when you rise up. You shall bind them as a sign on your hand, and they shall be as frontlets between your eyes. You shall write them on the doorposts of your house and on your gates (Deut. 6:4–9).

## Father and Fathers

As we seek to rebuild the broader culture through our churches and families, it is essential that the gospel light shines in the darkness and shows the way. There is, perhaps, no place where this is more needed than in the area of fatherhood. Sadly, the broader culture is an increasingly fatherless culture—an emasculated culture—to the point where father-hunger is one of the great needs of the day.

The more fatherless a culture is, the more dramatic the symptoms of the famine at both the macro- and the micro- levels. Father-love is the solution to the problem.

A pervasive fatherless culture has led us to our aimless, postmodern, emasculated culture: "Who's to say? Who's to lead? Who's to protect?" We are left without authority, guidance, or protection—all of these are fatherly provisions—and we are left empty and hungry. As Christian men desperately look for an image of a godly father and household, it is natural to look to the past. We find old images in books, and soon a movement is born that tries to recreate those nostalgic old images. As charming and quaint as they might seem, they are as out of place as three-cornered hats and buckled shoes. We end up looking silly and, worse, we become culturally irrelevant. We need to know what a father looks like *today*.

## Painting a New Image Using the
## Old Colors of Scripture

As we learn how to worship and how to live in a community, we learn how to pull together and how to live around the Table and around our tables. We have to start thinking again. This will take a self-conscious re-design. We are called to be fathers that truly represent "Our Father." This will feel awkward at first because in many respects it is new. Yet for our sons and daughters it will feel normal. We buy what is familiar. This is why advertisers spend millions on branding. What is feeding our imagination? It cannot feed on what it has not seen or heard. Pop-culture gives us father-images: buffoons and lovable idiots, the old fogey, the abusive father, and so forth. We begin with abstract knowledge: theology (what God thinks), followed by instruction and verbal images (preaching and teaching). Little by little the new pictures get drawn. Soon they become plausible; next, they become habit (culture); finally, they become generational.

## Fathers and the Gospel

The light of the gospel is the *only light*. So, as the gospel light shines through fathers, it soon shines through the family cultures. The darkness of the broader culture is thereby exposed and dispelled. Father-hunger is really the hunger for love. True love provides; it provides everything. The father's first duty is to love—to love first. "We love Him because He first loved us" (1 John 4:19). Central to love is giving or sacrificing for the sake of the beloved. John 3:16 sets this before us: "For God so loved the world that He gave His only begotten Son, that whoever believes in Him should not perish but have everlasting life." And so, earthly fathers—if they are to fill the emptiness—must likewise give of themselves, sacrifice themselves for the sake of their families. Since earthly fathers represent God the Father, loveless, hateful fathers produce resentment against God the Father, raising God-haters instead of God-lovers.

Our father Abraham was the pattern for godly father-hood. God had promised Abraham that He would "be God to you and your descendants after you," (Gen. 17:7), that He would make him a "great and mighty nation," (Gen. 18:18), and that "all the nations of the earth would be blessed in him" (Gen. 18:18). But God's covenant promises of blessing were conditioned upon Abraham and his descendants keeping the terms of the covenant (all a part of God's gracious work): "As for you, you shall keep My covenant, you and your descendants after you throughout their generations" (Gen. 17:9). We then read: "For I have known him [Abraham], in order that he may command his children and his household after him, that they keep the way of the LORD, to do righteousness and justice, that the LORD may bring to Abraham what He has spoken to him" (Gen. 18:19).

Notice the centrality of the condition of fatherly faithfulness: Abraham must personally keep covenant with God, and his descendants must keep covenant with God. The means of accomplishing this would be Abraham's commanding his children and household to keep the way of the Lord. All of this is the work of gospel grace in the life of a godly father.

## Logical and Analogical

God the Father is logical; we are analogical. It is, therefore, essential that we have before us the proper "form" of a father without allowing it to become "formalism" (form without substance). Fatherhood is always an issue of the heart; we cannot be simply technicians. We must be full of both wisdom and grace, self-consciously setting before the world a true image of God the Father. Through this we can change the world for many generations; this is the work of the gospel.

A word of caution for over-compensating fathers is, perhaps, needed. Men need not thump their chests, but rather recognize that when we are reclaiming some lost territory, balance is essential. In our rush to get out of the ditch on one side, we can easily fall into the ditch on the other side. Well-intentioned but over-zealous fathers can also leave children hungry. Force-feeding is not the solution. As image-bearers of the Father, we show the world what a father is supposed to look like. We are to be great lovers (i.e., great givers). It is a high standard, but when the question is asked about you as a father, one response should dominate: "He loves his family." And when the follow-up question comes—"How do you know?"—they say, "We see it in his sacrifice for his family's sake." He is there when they need him. He is there before they need him. He defends, he confronts, he feeds, he protects, he weeps, and he rejoices with them and for them. He never asks them to do what they haven't already seen him do. He is masculine, courageous, and loving; clear, resolute, wise, and gracious; imitating the heavenly Father in every way possible. This is where a Christian family culture begins.

## The Husbandman

The head, the husband, the father is not only the image bearer of God the Father and Christ the Husband, he is the *image setter* for the rest of the family culture (and ultimately the broader culture). Not only what he says, but more importantly, what he does will become the model for the rest of the household and future generations. He is the cultivator of the vineyard, and it is that cultivation (or lack thereof) that will be the basis of cultural fruitfulness (Prov. 24:30–34). If he is a man full of grace and godly character, he will act courageously with clear and resolute purpose, especially when no one else is looking. Like God, he is a man of his word; if he said he would do it, it is as good as done. A man who self-consciously and joyfully does his duty before God is respected by those who are under his care, and emulation of that character becomes the root of generational and cultural transformation. Like the heavenly Father, an earthly father is a provider and protector, but he must also be one with the vision to lead the family (by example) and to show them where they are going. Like Christ, he is the loving, sacrificing husband for his bride. And like the Holy Spirit, by his labor he manifests his true relationship with the Father and the Son. Christian family culture cannot develop and prosper without these clear images constantly being portrayed and reinforced. Families are outposts of the Church—the Kingdom of God—and fathers and husbands are building little cities at those outposts.

# Chapter 2
# Family and Worship
*Randy Booth*

## Introduction
*The Church*

The word "church" encompasses a great deal. The Church is an organism and an organization. We "go to church" and we are the Church. We sit in the church and we don't run in the church, and yet the "Church is invisible." The Church is *one* and the Church is *many*. It has a history and a future. It's both universal and local. The Church is a "body," a "bride," a "flock," an "olive tree," and a "household." We "join churches," and we "leave churches." The Church is militant and it is eschatological. And there's much more that we can say about the Church.

God has placed His Church at the *center* and *summit* of the world. The Church is comprised of the people of God called out of the world into union with the crucified and risen Lord. As God's people, His new humanity, we are an outpost of heaven on earth. We are marked out by baptism in the Triune name.

We gather around His Table to feast. And we declare our common faith in Jesus Christ, who is now seated at the Father's right hand in heaven as King of kings and Lord of lords. The Lord Jesus Christ rules over all things for the

sake of the Church (Eph. 1:22–23), which in turn exists
for the sake of the world. Calvin writes:

> Because it is now our intention to discuss the
> visible church, let us learn from the simple title
> "mother" how useful, indeed how necessary, it
> is that we should know her. For there is no other
> way to enter into life unless this mother conceive
> us in her womb, give us birth, nourish us at her
> breast, and lastly, unless she keep us under her
> care and guidance until, putting off mortal flesh,
> we become like the angels. Our weakness does
> not allow us to be dismissed from her school until
> we have been pupils all our lives (*Institutes* 4.1.4).[11]

We have formally vowed, before God and one another,
to be united to the Church of Jesus Christ. We have said,
"I do," in obedience to the Word of God, uniting ourselves
with this body of believers, in submission to the elders and
to one another, for service to those who are of the household of faith, and for the advancement of the kingdom of
Christ. Many have devalued the Church. It is devalued by
corruption within—involving both leadership and laity. It
is devalued by a lack of understanding of her importance
and place in the world and in the life of God's people. It
has been trivialized by shallowness and silliness. It has been
compromised by seeking the approval of the world. Indeed,
it is thought of as "optional" by many individual Christians
who can take-it-or-leave it since they feel no real sense of
obligation to the Church. But the Bible teaches us that the

---

[1] John Calvin, *The Institutes of the Christian Religion*, 2 vols., trans. Ford
Lewis Battles, ed. John Thomas McNeil (Philadelphia: Westminster, 1993).

Church is the center of the world, the nursery of Christ's kingdom. It is *the most important institution on earth* because it is the people of God, *"the pillar and ground of the truth"* (1 Tim. 3:15). With the Church and through the Church, societies live and die, rise and fall.

### A "Family-Friendly Church"

We've heard a good bit in the last few years about the "family-friendly church." Perhaps the "Family-Life Center" provides the most tangible picture of this modern emphasis. What can the Church do for you and your family?

Now we do not want "Family-Unfriendly" churches. Certainly, there is a genuine need for churches to be concerned with ministering to the needs of families. However, terminology can, and often does, point us in the wrong direction. It is a matter of priorities. Taken by itself, such terminology can be dangerous because what it presents is only a partial truth. This perspective can push people to view the Church as an auxiliary institution. The Church's purpose then becomes that of assisting the family. Soon the family is viewed as the *primary* institution of life in the world. I'm suggesting that we do need a "focus on the family," but the family that needs our focus is the family we call the Church. With a proper view of the place of the Church, we will develop a better and stronger view of our individual families. Remember, our call to follow Christ involves self-denial and even a denial of family relationships.

Once Christ becomes central, then we can *return* to ourselves, our families, and our things with a proper perspective—they all serve Him. Mother Church feeds and nourishes us as we gather around the Father's Table. From there, we are sent out to serve.

*The "Church-Friendly Family"*

A better emphasis is needed. We must come to see the Church as the *primary family* and our individual families as *outposts* of the Church. I recently had the privilege of baptizing my eighth grandchild, Henry. My son and his wife handed their child over to Jesus (and His Church). After he was baptized, Jesus handed him back to his parents to take him home and raise him in the fear and admonition of the Lord. In our individual families we serve the larger—the primary—family. We are sent out to serve the Body of Christ and the world, and we come back on the first day of every week to gather around the Family Table. The Apostle Paul speaks of this ecclesiastical unity with these words:

> Now, therefore, you are no longer strangers and foreigners, but fellow citizens with the saints and members of the household of God, having been built on the foundation of the apostles and prophets, Jesus Christ Himself being the chief corner stone, in whom the whole building, being joined together, grows into a holy temple in the Lord, in whom you also are being built together for a dwelling place of God in the Spirit (Eph. 2:19–22).

The Church, then, is the *primary institution of society*. If the Church is the household, family, and kingdom of God, then we must see that the individual families serve the Church.

*Worship of the True God*

Worship of God is the true center of every society. God cannot be worshiped rightly in any culture without that worship challenging and dislocating all idolatries. To focus on the right worship of God is to declare war; it is to throw down the gauntlet. We must be sure that we acknowledge the priority of God's claim.

The problem we have been facing in recent years is that we don't really view the Church as the primary family from which every other family draws its name. The Church is not an institution ordained to assist the family so that *it* does the work of the kingdom. It's the other way round: the family is an institution that is utterly dependent upon the Church in order to be equipped and guided so that it can be a blessing to the world rather than a curse (which, apart from the Church, every family would be). The same is true for the State. The Church holds the place of primacy—always. If it is the Body of Christ, then there's no other place for it.

## Communion

*Living in Communion with Him and with Others*

The Fall wrecked this arrangement. The Church, however, is the place where we are restored and then sent out to live. Every person, every family, has its trials and pains. We sometimes think our own difficulties are unparalleled, but this kind of thinking would only indicate how little we get out and how shallow our knowledge of others really is. God calls us to live, and He calls us to live in the context of the community of His people. To the degree we forsake that assembly with our bodies or our hearts, our suffering will increase. It's in the covenant community where we are honed and polished. We learn to serve and to be longsuffering; we learn to forgive and love, and we learn how to deny ourselves and how to be blessed by others.

In Acts 2, every day believers met together in the Temple courts, broke bread in one another's homes, and ate together with glad and sincere hearts. Hebrews 3:13 suggests that many years later, Christians were still meeting daily. For this to become a part of our daily living we must develop covenant consciousness; this is a way of thinking that begins with the congregation rather than the individual—that is, thinking in terms of "we" instead of "me." It's in the context of the covenant community that we find rest and restoration. The way we develop the covenant community mindset begins by believing and obeying our loving heavenly Father. We must resist the temptation to withdraw and, instead, do our duty. Our duty is to trust and obey even when we don't feel like it.

We have all taken public vows before God and His people to be committed participants in the covenant community we call *church*. The Church is not a spectator sport. You are here to serve. The question of how often you decide to go to the church should essentially be a one-time decision. There is nothing you do every week that is more important than participating in corporate worship.

Here are a few important points for us to remember if we are to comprehend and implement life in the Christian community so that we and our families will know the blessings of God for many generations:

*The Lord's Day*: "Remember the Sabbath day, to keep it holy…" (Exod. 20:8). This day distinguishes the covenant people of God from the world.

*Worship*: "Not forsaking the assembling of ourselves together…" (Heb. 10:25). The corporate worship of the one true God is central to the covenant community.

*Fellowship*: "As iron sharpens iron, so one man sharpens the countenance of his friend" (Prov. 27:17). If we are not in the homes of other church members, and other church members are not in our homes, then we cannot possibly know one another the way we should.

*Time management*: "Seek first the kingdom of God and His righteousness, and all these things shall be added to you" (Matt. 6:33). We cannot manage time, but we can manage ourselves. When we become so busy with work or other activities, that we begin to neglect our families and our covenant community, then our orientation is not covenantal, but has become misdirected. Maintaining covenant priorities requires constant vigilance.

*Communication*: Our identity as a called people is strengthened by our common interests. We are called to pray for one another and to teach and admonish one another.

*Geography*: "Let us do good to all, especially to those who are of the household of faith" (Gal. 6:10). Daily interaction among our fellow Christians provides abundant opportunities to love one another.

### Trinity and Community

The Trinity is a community of persons, and thus man himself, being created in the image of God, thrives only in community. Unlike God, however, no man is complete in himself or equal to other men. We are dependent creatures, dependent not only on our Creator, but also on other creatures. None of us possesses all the attributes of human nature in the same degree. We are individuals who must live in society with other individuals if we are to know the fullness of life. Others fill up what we lack. You need to be ten percent more like your fellow church members. You have something to learn from every single member.

Sin introduced enmity between God and man and thereby ruptured the community or communion so that to be cut off from that community is death. Man has been hiding from God (and from other men) ever since. Therefore, God (by His grace) intervened by way of the Mediator, reconciling the world to himself, and now man can finally come out of hiding and return to the Father's Table. "For if by the one man's offense death reigned through the one, much more those who receive abundance of grace and of the gift of righteousness will reign in life through the One, Jesus Christ" (Rom. 5:17).

By faith in Christ we are reunited with the Triune God and thus brought back into the original society. By our baptism we are engrafted into the Body of Christ and thus joined to the community of other men where we can serve and be served, love and be loved. It is in the context of this covenant with Christ and His Church that we find the fulfillment of His promise: abundant life. We die alone. We live together!

### Respect and Community

One of the serious deficits in the broader culture is that people are oblivious to others—it's all about "me." We see this in the way people talk, walk, dress, drive, and so forth. This has seeped into the Church, and, under the guise of "accepting people the way they are," we have allowed them to continue to be the way they are, and thus we contribute to the atrophy of the culture. People come to church, or come late, or fellowship, or serve, or give, or worship, or participate *if they feel like it*, never considering how this impacts the community. Children have often grown up with this apathy toward others. It is the epitome of immaturity.

### Worship and the Family

I don't so much want to address family worship as I want to address corporate worship and the family.

Family worship is an extension of the Church's corporate worship; it doesn't stand alone. The same is true for individual worship. The worship of the congregation is central or primary, and the failure to understand this has diminished the influence of the Church in the culture.

The Church is the worshiping community; she is the hub, and our families are the spokes. We are called to serve the Body of Christ. In serving Christ first, we are also served (as a part of the Body). But the Church doesn't exist to serve me first. It's the Church that teaches us how to worship and, therefore, how to live. We begin the first day of each week gathered together as the household of God in preparation for life.

We should think of the Lord's Day worship as practice for life. It provides a blueprint—an image—of how to live. We are not simply "doing the liturgy," we are learning to "live the liturgy." Every church has a liturgy (i.e., an order), and that liturgy does ultimately get lived out. We learn to come when God calls us and to listen to Him when He speaks. We learn to respond with gratitude and thankfulness in our hearts. We practice prayer and the confession of our sins and are reminded of God's gracious pardon and absolution. We have the privilege of giving cheerfully and of offering up songs of praise. We learn to receive

instruction through the Word preached and to remember
our confession of what we believe. This all culminates in
a gathering around the family Table in communion. And
after we practice, we are sent out (with God's benediction)
to go to our homes and do it all over again every day of
the week.

*The Centrality of Worship*

Everyone worships someone or something. Everyone
reflects that worship in how he lives.

It' is in our corporate worship that we are shaped together—we are shaped in communion. This is where and
how a culture is built. There are common ideas and beliefs
and practices. In other words, we have communion. Again,
Paul summarizes this glorious communion in Ephesians:

> And He Himself gave some to be apostles, some
> prophets, some evangelists, and some pastors and
> teachers, for the equipping of the saints for the
> work of ministry, for the edifying of the body of
> Christ, till we all come to the unity of the faith
> and of the knowledge of the Son of God, to a
> perfect man, to the measure of the stature of the
> fullness of Christ; that we should no longer be
> children, tossed to and fro and carried about with
> every wind of doctrine, by the trickery of men,
> in the cunning craftiness of deceitful plotting,
> but, speaking the truth in love, may grow up in all
> things into Him who is the head—Christ—from
> whom the whole body, joined and knit together by
> what every joint supplies, according to the effective
> working by which every part does its share, causes

growth of the body for the edifying of itself in love (Eph. 4:11–16).

Our worship establishes our views and our relationships to God, ourselves, our families, our neighbors, our possessions, and our time. Moreover, worship is always the most central fact about a culture. Every religion vies for power and control of our culture. At the center of every culture is the worship of that culture's God. And so I ask you, which god is our broader culture worshiping, and do you see any parallels in how the Church is worshiping?

If people worship God according to His Word—if they have a consciousness of following His Word in their worship—then their culture will reflect that. For if we honor the Lord in His worship—being careful to follow His Word then we would expect the same people to take heed to His Word elsewhere. But if we ignore His Word in His worship, then we will ignore His Word elsewhere. If we will ignore His Word in that one activity that is directly related to His glory, we will not have any conscience about following His Word *particularly* in any other area of life.

So you see, how we worship determines the very nature of the culture that we, as a people, build (family culture and broader culture). A departure from the true God begins when we fail to worship Him properly. This will be seen in a casual, flippant, or heartless worship. Then it will be seen in the abandonment of God's worship—forsaking the Lord's Day (or Sabbath) altogether.

### Worship as Cultural Warfare

It is us and our God against them and their god. All wars, including culture wars, are religious wars. This is why

Rome had a Pantheon (a temple dedicated to all the gods). Every time a new state was absorbed by Rome, their god went into the Pantheon because it was an alliance. You have to embrace them *and their god*. This led to the warfare between Rome and the Church. The Christians were willing to be good citizens of Rome, but they couldn't acknowledge the other gods of the Empire. This made Christians political traitors. Christians were killed because of their treason. They were denying the theology of the Empire. Thus, worship is warfare. It's where we are equipped and trained. It's the place from where we are sent out to serve. Because of its centrality, if you neglect or forsake corporate worship, you will lose your liberty. True freedom comes from obedience to the true God; so true worship is central to all of life. When we start fiddling with this, we are fiddling with the world. Worship has consequences. How you worship directly impacts your life and those around you—especially your family. Every Sunday you send a message to your family (and ultimately to the world) as to what your priorities are. You tell everyone who your God is.

Formal worship is a time when we remind ourselves of our constant and standing duties in the light of who God is. On the Lord's Day, our worship reminds us that the rest of the week belongs to Him as well. We're not setting aside God's portion of the week, but are reminding the entire family that the entire day and the entire week is His. Put another way, formal worship doesn't create a secular/ sacred distinction. Understood in the classic Protestant fashion, it obliterates it. We give one day in seven because all seven are His. We give ten percent because one hundred percent is His.

## Conclusion

As our culture is tossed to and fro by every wind of doctrine, and taken captive by many novel notions, faithfulness to the authoritative Word of God—defended and boldly declared—remains as our great mission. The Church is God's ark, the place of safety, preservation, and victory. We are "the pillar and ground of the truth" (1 Tim. 3:15). The apostle Paul admonished Timothy to "be ready in season and out of season. Convince, rebuke, exhort, with all longsuffering and teaching" (2 Tim. 4:2). He was not referring to Timothy's personal ups and downs. He was referring to the culture around him—both inside and outside the Church. Our steadfast worship of the Triune God is critical to victory. "The horse is prepared for the day of battle, but deliverance is of the LORD" (Prov. 21:31). A "Church-Friendly Family" is the path to transforming our culture.

# Chapter 3
# Family and Education
*Randy Booth*

I presume that most, if not all of you, are persuaded of the absolute necessity of Christian education. I suspect that many of you have been fully engaged in the process either through home schooling, online classes, or Christian day schools. I am sure you are familiar with the various intramural debates over curriculum and methods. The amount of materials and training is enormous, and the quality of the material is constantly improving. My wife and I began home schooling twenty-five years ago and we are now watching our children educate our grandchildren. I have been the founding board chairman of two Classical Christian Schools. I have lectured at numerous education conferences and produced a series on "The Necessity of a Christian Education." So, what can I say to you that is not old news?

## How Are We Doing After 25 Years?

Where are the gaps, and where does our focus need to be now? There is certainly much to commend. Nevertheless, there is much left to do. Education is far more than a good curriculum and organization. If you have been at this for very long, you know that the ideals and the realities are often far apart. And the frustrations and disappointments can be overwhelming at times. If our goals are unclear, then it is possible that our labor could be (at least partly) in vain. Jesus asked, "For what profit is it to a man if he gains the whole world, and is himself destroyed or lost?"(Luke 9:25). What kind of children does God want? That is the question. What would His "report card" look like?

## Someone's Religion Controls

Every religion vies for power and control of our culture, and everyone has a religion. One of the most useful tools in the quest for power over the lives of men is found in the educational system. John Kenneth Galbraith regards it as the successor to land and capital as the most important determinant of who controls whom.[1] George Orwell observed in his novel, *1984*: "Who controls the past controls the future; who controls the present controls the past."[2] Understanding that whoever has power over the mind has power over the culture, Orwell had one of his characters declare: "The Party is not interested in the overt act: the thought is all we care about. We do not merely destroy our enemies; we change them."[3] Author Herbert Schlossberg observes that "Education is a series of religious acts in part because the power of assumption is so great. Assumptions, in fact, are more powerful than assertions, because they bypass the critical faculty and thereby create prejudice." Government education assumes God to be irrelevant to the educational process when, in fact, "The fear of the

---

[1] John Kenneth Galbraith, *The New Industrial State* (Boston: Houghton Mifflin, 1967; reprinted, Princeton, NJ: Princeton University Press, 2007), 302.

[2] George Orwell, *1984* (New York: Harcourt Brace, 1949; reprinted, New York: Penguin, 2003), 35–36.

[3] Orwell, *1984*, 261.

LORD is the beginning of knowledge" (Prov. 1:7). Such false assumptions by the government schools can then be combined with arguments that prove "the truth of what is false. The false assumption is additionally beguiling because it often appeals to one of the worst instincts—the desire to be fashionable or at least to avoid being associated with the unfashionable or unpopular."[4]

## The Biblical Goal of Education

We read in Malachi 2:15, "But did He not make them [husband and wife] one, having a remnant of the Spirit? And why one? He seeks godly offspring. Therefore take heed to your spirit. . . ." God's purpose is to fill the earth with godly people, and, therefore, this must be *our* goal in educating our children.

Education provides the tools, and those tools will be in the hands of someone who can use them for good or ill. Good tools must be in the hands of good men and women. Good tools in the hands of those who do not serve Christ are dangerous. Indeed, their spiritual condition and the content of their character are far more essential than a high G.P.A.

The Proverbs set up a clear contrast between the wise and the foolish. The Bible starts with the assumptions that "Foolishness is bound up in the heart of a child," (Prov. 22:15) and "The fear of the LORD is the beginning of wisdom" (Prov. 1:7). I have known some very smart fools. I have also known many who struggled academically but who have shown themselves to be very wise.

---

[4] Herbert Schlossberg, *Idols for Destruction: The Conflict of Christian Faith and American Culture* (Nashville, TN: Thomas Nelson, 1983; reprinted, Wheaton: Crossway, 1993), 210–211.

True wisdom is the biblical goal of education, and biblical wisdom has certain characteristics that are essential: it has ethical content that is rooted in the truth and authority of God's Word. Biblical wisdom is humble, and humility in turn is gracious and grateful. Biblical wisdom manifests the fruit of the Spirit: "love, joy, peace, longsuffering, kindness, goodness, faithfulness, gentleness, self-control" (Gal. 5:22–23a). At the end of the day, if your family is not filled with a good bit of joy, laughter, kindness, and respect, then the education you are providing is insufficient and flawed.

## The Sower and the Seed

In the parable of the Sower and the Seed, Jesus describes the various soils the seed fell upon. His description of the "good ground" shocked me the first time I noticed it: "But the ones [seed] that fell on the good ground are those who, having heard the word with a *noble and good heart*, keep it and bear fruit with patience" (Luke 8:15).Where did these "noble and good hearts" come from? I would contend that, by and large, they were the hearts that were cultivated by godly parents.

## Cultural Transmission

Parents represent God. As I pointed out previously, as Christian parents you have handed your children over to Jesus (in baptism), and He handed them back to you to raise for Him. You are Christ's representatives to your children. From you, they will receive an education about justice and mercy, law and love, truth and beauty, loyalty and sacrifice, and everything else that is important in life. An education that is void of these things is of little value. God is (or should be) the environment of your child—constant and total. As the Church equips the saints for service, parents (and their agents), who are outposts of the Church, must also equip their children for service in the kingdom of God.

A comprehensive and unified Christian view and way of life is, therefore, what God requires of parents and their agents. Parents are responsible for the kind of worldview their children are taught and for the kind of instruction they receive in specific subjects.

> This Book of the Law shall not depart from your mouth, but you shall meditate in it day and night, that you may observe to do according to all that is written in it. For then you will make your way prosperous, and then you will have good success (Josh. 1:8).

It is not enough to believe that the education of the home and the school must be Christian. It is one thing to have a general belief concerning how things should be. It is another matter altogether to be able to articulate that belief and able to persuade others of its necessity as well. Your calling is to *inculcate*—that is, to internalize—in your children affection for the things of God. In order to do that, your heart must first be turned toward them, and, in turn, their hearts will be inclined toward you. No check-box system can possibly produce the kind of children God calls us to educate.

Now I hope that more and more Christians are realizing that there is, in fact, no neutral ground in education or anywhere else. Nothing can be taught apart from some religious presupposition. Certainly, some parents home school or place their children in Christian schools in hopes of avoiding drugs, sex, violence, disease, and so forth. But the purpose for Christian education is not to facilitate flight from the surface symptoms, but to counteract the source of that infection. Only an education that is self-consciously Christian and full-orbed is equipped to provide a moral and academically competent education for our children. We must provide the hothouse that prepares students for the harsh warfare of a world that is hostile toward God. Ignorance and innocence are not the same thing. We are not protecting our children in the long run by shielding them from the world.

God has called us to teach them how to live in *this world* in *this century*. Schools are central in the transmission of a culture. A worldview is exactly what a child is given in school. We must understand the strategic importance of the current educational establishment in the re-paganization of our current culture. If we are to have a truly Christian culture, it is essential that we have a self-consciously Christian education at every level and in every field of study producing *godly* men and women that adorn the gospel of Jesus Christ. Again, this is an extension of the work of the Church through our families. Families, in turn, educate children for Christ.

## Nurture in the Lord

Christian *nurture* is at the heart of true Christian education.

> Behold, I will send you Elijah the prophet before the coming of the great and dreadful day of the LORD. And he will turn the hearts of the fathers to the children, and the hearts of the children to

their fathers, lest I come and strike the earth with a curse (Mal. 4:5–6).

We seek to *win the heart* of the child, and we only do that when our hearts are directed toward them. If you do not have a heart for your child or your students, then there cannot be a Christian culture. We love them in spite of themselves. The goal of all our instruction is to help them—to reprove, rebuke, exhort, with all longsuffering. Our call is to shape the ideal man, who would be able to take his place in the ideal culture. Moreover, the goal of our education is to bring that culture about. We are here to accomplish nothing less than the enculturation of the future citizen. So then, education is not just a bound curriculum, it is enculturation—every aspect of enculturation.

The Bible tells us to bring up our children in the nurture and admonition of the Lord (Eph. 6:4). The Lord Jesus Christ tells us to love the Lord our God with all our heart, with all our soul, and with all our mind (Matt. 22:37). The many years that are devoted to formal education greatly impact the direction and thoughts of our children. Parents desire their children's success intellectually, socially, and physically, but most important for the Christian parent is their child's understanding and application of the Christian faith. Providing Christian education for our children is costly, but not nearly as costly as the alternatives. Problems in modern American society and education are frightening to parents. Christians should not be surprised at these problems since they are the expected result of a culture that rejects God. But Christians should not panic and retreat. Jesus said, "In the world you will have tribulation; but be of good cheer, I have overcome the world" (John 16:33).

It is with assurance of Christ's victory that we labor each day. Education is to be conducted in light of God's revelation of himself in the Scriptures and in recognition that all truth is God's truth.

We seek to raise a high standard for both Christian character and academic achievement. We are committed to a biblical worldview in all areas of life; therefore, we want to teach children how God's Word and world relate to all subject areas. Your commitment to provide the spiritual and academic benefits of a Christian education will affect your children and students for this world and for eternity. Furthermore, it will affect the future of our civilization. Christian education is not simply a luxury when we consider our responsibilities toward God. Children from Christian homes must learn to "think God's thoughts after Him" and to view all facts as God-created, God-controlled facts. The sacrifices that are made will be blessed by God. You are always teaching and children are always learning. There are no genuinely "private acts."We are always connected to the community. Our attitudes, words, and behavior constantly impact others and, indeed, the entire educational culture. This is a critical lesson for us and our children to learn: the process of imitation. The Apostle Paul wrote: "Imitate me, just as I also imitate Christ" (1 Cor. 11:1). A familial approach to education is, therefore, essential. This means you and your students love God with all your heart, soul, mind, and strength. This means you love your students.

This means you insist on your students loving you and loving the others around them. It means love is at the core of any genuine education. Love is demonstrated by obedience. Jesus said, "If you love Me, keep my commandments." Rebellion is the opposite of love. Love is doing for someone what they need, not necessarily what they want. The overly indulged do not know how to honor and respect. The attitude is: "You owe me." The nurtured and disciplined know how to deny themselves and how to give to others.

## Of First Importance

The most important lesson a child can learn is the lesson of respect. In fact, honor and respect are the *only* rules. All other rules are sub-rules of these. "Children, obey your parents in the Lord, for this is right. 'Honor your father and mother,' which is the first commandment with promise: 'that it may be well with you and you may live long on the earth'" (Eph. 6:1–3). This respect is shown in three fundamental ways:

(1) *Attitudes*: There can be no true honor if there is not first a godly attitude.

Rebellion is first nurtured in the heart—it is the product of sinful pride. "Nobody is going to tell me what to do!" Jesus quotes the prophet Isaiah saying, "These people . . . honor me with their lips, but their heart is far from Me" (Matt. 15:8). Children must show, *and must be required by their parents and teachers* to show, respectful attitudes toward their own parents and toward all those who hold superior positions over them, which is almost everyone. They should also display proper attitudes of respect toward their equals.

(2) *Words*: Parental authority must be honored and obeyed with the child's words and body language. Children must be trained to use the appropriate language of respect when addressing or responding to their parents (and other adults). When a child is permitted to use disrespectful language or to ignore the adult who is speaking to him, this

is a form of dishonor and disobedience. Furthermore, the Scriptures teach us that we are to pray for those in authority over us, which would include our parents and teachers: "Therefore I exort first of all that supplications, prayers, intercessions, and giving of thanks be made for all men, for kings and all who are in authority, that we may lead a quiet and peaceable life in all godliness and reverence" (1 Tim. 2:1–2).

(3) *Behavior:* Children show honor by their actions. Submission, respect, and obedience are demonstrated in what we do. "Eye-service" alone is not sufficient to honor those whom God has placed in authority over us. When we obey our parents and other legitimate authorities, we not only honor them, we honor God. This principle is taught in Colossians 3:22–24: "Bondservants, obey in all things your masters according to the flesh; not with eyeservice, as men-pleasers, but in sincerity of heart, fearing God. And whatever you do, do it heartily, as to the Lord, and not to men, knowing that from the Lord you will receive the reward of the inheritance; for you serve the Lord Christ."

## In Him We Live and Move and Have Our Being

God is our educational environment. He is imminent (present in all His fullness). "The fear of the LORD is the beginning of knowledge: but fools despise wisdom and instruction" (Prov. 1:7). Therefore, cultivating an awareness of His presence in our children is essential (the "fear of the Lord" and the "joy of the Lord"). We accomplish this task also through free interjection of God and His thought into lessons and conversations (Deut. 6) and through questions that necessitate the invocation of God and His thought

(His thoughts and ways are not naturally our thoughts and ways). Belief and unbelief are mutually exclusive—neither allows any room for the other.

Cornelius Van Til writes:

> All of us must stand together as one man. In this day when boundaries between the believer and the unbeliever are so generally wiped away we should seek to mark those boundaries anew and mark them well. We should seek to mark these boundaries not with chalk that disappears with the first rainstorm that comes, but we should try to mark these boundaries with indelible ink on the hearts of those who believe.[5]

And he adds:

> And anyone who comes to grips with it at all will sense the impossibility of thinking of Christian education as being ninety or sixty or thirty or ten percent like other education, the only difference being that Christian education adds certain elements or emphasizes certain elements that secular education neglects. When viewed from this absolute standpoint Christian education is not even a fraction of one percent like public education. The different conceptions of God that underlie the two theories cover every point on the whole front and cover them before and behind, without and within.[6]

[5] Cornelius Van Til, *Essays on Christian Education* (Phillipsburg, NJ: Presbyterian & Reformed, 1979), 166.

[6] Van Til, *Christian Education*, 189.

## Education is a Community Affair

Unfortunately, the community has often failed. As a result, we no longer trust one another. We have often retreated to try and do it our own way. This must change. Some have viewed the Christian school or home school as a place to retreat from a corrupt culture and secular education, a place to shelter our children from the harsh realities of modern culture. They become retreats from the world while we wait for the return of Christ to rescue us. Students are sheltered and often naive. The antithesis to this is seen in the few Christians who recognize the need for Christian education to be a boot camp that prepares children for service in the world. Rather than retreating from the culture, children are prepared to conquer the culture for Christ. They are exposed to a wide variety of things from the culture in the context of a distinctively Christian philosophy of education. They are given the tools of learning that will serve them for a lifetime.

## The Church Is the Hub of Our Community

Our families and the education of our children must be in the context of a covenant community, the Church. I am not saying the school must be governed directly by the Church, but neither should they be disconnected. While we might recognize the fact that our secular culture and schools are falling apart, there is apparently little recognition that our evangelical culture has similar problems. The modern Church often does not have a distinctive Christian worldview either—it has no epistemological center. Until families are oriented first toward the Body of Christ, most Christian schools and home schools will continue to reflect the superficial nature of the modern evangelical faith.

Christian schools are a cultural manifestation of a particular Christian subculture. If that subculture is in crisis, then the education of the children will reflect it.

## A Few Comments about Schools and Home-Schools

*Christian School vs. Christian Home School*

If we recognize that the Church is the center of the community, we will all be well served. Yet I see the insecurities, the strife, the jealousy, and the party spirit. But we are on the same team. This is not a competition. Even our striving should help us all to grow. It is really helpful if we will all admit that none of us have arrived yet. We are all doing some things wrong. We all need help and encouragement. We all need criticism. I see great successes and great disasters all around us. Adam and Eve home schooled with mixed results. Of course, they really did not have many options. All of our efforts at Christian education require an enormous amount of God's grace. You are not capable of giving your children the education God requires—not alone. Even the best families need the grace of God because even the best families fall short at many points.

The best schools are loaded with problems because they are loaded with sinners. I am a fan of all kinds of Christian education, but I am not a fan of every Christian school or every home school. I have done both, and I have succeeded and failed at both. We have to be willing to say that and believe it.

*Problems*

As a movement, home schooling has some serious problems. If that statement shifts you immediately into "defensive mode," then that is the first problem. Christian schools have at least as many problems as home schools, but they also have an abundance of critics to have to deal with on a daily basis. The sooner we all face the fact that we are needy—that we need God and the Church, and we need each other—the better off we will be.

All "movements" tend to produce extremes. Movements are usually reacting to some failure in the current system. We often do not have many choices. Reactions tend to be over-reactions. And so, the pendulum swings too far in the opposite direction.

Moreover, movements tend to attract extreme personalities, and thus, the "super-home schooler" is born. Every detail is absolutized, from the kind of bran that should be in your breakfast muffins to the exact list of books that must be read. These well-intentioned personalities tend to drive a movement, rolling over whoever gets in their way. This produces feelings of inadequacy in those who cannot quite live up to the standard. It also gives the movement a black eye, as others now react to this overreaction. Movements can easily latch on to ignorance and to well-intentioned enthusiasm, elevating some things to a legalistic level, tying the shoelaces very tight. Among some—remember, I am speaking in very broad categories—there have been some monastic tendencies.

*A Withdrawal from Society into a Unique Subculture*

Rather than remaining in the world, there is a gnostic tendency to create an alternative world. We are called to be salt and light in the world where God has placed us. As Christians, we cannot possibly reach a world with which we have no contact. As the late Dutch theologian, Abraham Kuyper, wrote:

Far more precious to us than even the development of human life, is the crown which ennobles it, and this noble crown of life for you and me rests in the Christian name. That crown is our common heritage. It was not from Greece or Rome that the regeneration of human life came forth;—that mighty metamorphosis dates from Bethlehem and Golgotha. . . . But, in deadly opposition to this Christian element, against the very Christian name, and against its salutiferous influence in every sphere of life, the storm of Modernism has now arisen with violent intensity. . . . There is no doubt then that Christianity is imperilled by great and serious dangers. Two *life-systems* are wrestling with one another, in mortal combat. . . . If the battle is to be fought with honor and with a hope of victory, then *principle* must be arrayed against *principle*; then it must be felt that in Modernism the vast energy of an all-embracing *life-system* assails us, then also it must be understood that we have to take our stand in a life-system of equally comprehensive and far-reaching power.[7]

---

[7] Abraham Kuyper, *Lectures on Calvinism* (reprint, Grand Rapids: Eerdmans, 1987), 10–11.

# Chapter 4
# The Family Table
*Randy Booth*

## God Prepares a Table for Us

¹ The LORD is my shepherd;
   I shall not want.
² He makes me to lie down in green pastures;
   He leads me beside the still waters.
³ He restores my soul;
   He leads me in the paths of righteousness
   For His name's sake.
⁴ Yea, though I walk through the valley of the
      shadow of death,
   I will fear no evil;
   For You are with me;
   Your rod and Your staff, they comfort me.
⁵ You prepare a table before me in the presence of
      my enemies;
   You anoint my head with oil;
   My cup runs over.
⁶ Surely goodness and mercy shall follow me
   All the days of my life;
   And I will dwell in the house of the LORD forever.
                              —Psalm 23

*The Liturgy Is Practice for Life*

We start the first day of each week gathered at the family table to renew our strength in preparation for the week ahead. We are not *doing* the liturgy. Rather, we are preparing to *live* the liturgy. This is why there is nothing we do each week that is more important than worship. Gathering at a particular place (the Table) with a particular people (the household of God), we are sent forth to live with fresh focus on life (covenant-renewal).

*The Profundity of the Lord's Table*

There has always been a close link between the Church's understanding of the nature of the sacrament and the attention she gives to it. Use tends to follow perceived significance. If something does not mean much then we would expect to see it used very little. When the communion table is neglected, the people of God are malnourished. What a man thinks of the Lord's Table is a clear indication of what he will think of Christ, the Church, and theology itself.

R. C. Sproul writes: "The light of the sacrament of the Lord's Supper is in eclipse. The shadows of postmodern relativism have covered the Table. For the Lord's Supper to be restored to the spiritual life of the church there must be an awakening to its meaning, significance, and power."[11]

John Calvin elaborates on the significance of the Lord's Table:

---

[1] R. C. Sproul, "Foreword," in Keith A. Mathison, *Given for You: Reclaiming Calvin's Doctrine of the Lord's Supper* (Phillipsburg, NJ: P&R, 2002), x.

God has received us, once for all, into his family, to hold us not only as servants but as sons. Thereafter, to fulfill the duties of a most excellent Father concerned for his offspring, he undertakes also to nourish us throughout the course of our life. And not content with this alone, he has willed, by giving his pledge, to assure us of this continuing liberality. To this end, therefore, he has, through the hand of his only-begotten Son, given to his church another sacrament, that is, a spiritual banquet, wherein Christ attests himself to be the life-giving bread, upon which our souls feed unto true and blessed immortality... The signs are bread and wine, which represent for us the invisible food we receive from the flesh and blood of Christ... Now Christ is the only food of our soul, and therefore our Heavenly Father invites us to Christ, that, refreshed by partaking of him, we may repeatedly gather strength until we shall have reached heavenly immortality (*Inst.* 4.17.1).

Since the Table is diminished and disappearing from the Church, it is also diminishing and disappearing from our homes. The two are connected. Fast-food and drive-thrus have replaced the family table.

This follows in the wake of "seeker-friendly" worship and a casual view of the Lord's Table; eating together around a table used to mean something.

### The Lord's Table is the Archetype of our Family Tables

Or perhaps we should say that our family tables *should* be an imitation or reflection of the Lord's Table. Remember, liturgy is life—what we do here means something. It sends a message. It teaches a lesson.

We come to the Lord's Table each Lord's Day to be fed by the Father, who meets our needs above and beyond all that we could ask or think. He has given us life. He sustains that life. He protects that life. The Table is the very image of fatherhood, the essence of which is love.

We begin each week gathered around the Table as children to be instructed and nourished just before we are sent out to live. And so, too, we go to our homes and gather around smaller tables to be instructed and nourished, and from there we also fan out to live and to love. The liturgy is practice for life.

The Lord's Table has many metaphors by which we see the depth and simplicity of God's work. We see the seriousness of our sin and the magnitude of Christ's sacrifice, the grace of God in giving His Son, the peace that is made between us and Him, the power of the resurrection, the declaration of His death (and all its implications), the hope of His return, and the communion of saints. It's a simple picture of the gospel, so simple that a child can understand. It's an appeal to all five senses. It's the image of the intimacy of the Groom and His bride (not unlike the marriage bed).

It's the family Table, where we receive food, nourishment, and joy, and where we share and serve, and we are served. It's the place of gratitude and thanksgiving. It's all of this and much more. It's both light and deep. The Table is the geographic center of the Church and the home. The Table is so profound that it encompasses every dimension of our lives, and, therefore, a variety of descriptions and expressions are appropriate. Every trip to the Table should be exciting, enlightening, and renewing, but they don't all have to be exactly alike.

## A Prepared Table
*A Table in the Presence of our Enemies*

There is a curious mystery that does battle in my mind. On the one hand, we live in a world full of sin and misery. Think of the multitude of individual sins—ours and others—along with all their minor and major consequences; the pain and suffering of sickness, injury, and death; the sadness of weariness and loss. This world is a very ugly place. On the other hand, as Christians, we at the same time live in a world wholly unlike the one I just described. God's Word tells us to live with contentment and even joy in the midst of these very trials. We are called to rejoice in and for all things—all the imperfect things.

In the midst of the ugliness of a fallen world, we are instructed to see with different eyes and hear with different ears: "Finally, brethren, whatever things are true, whatever things are noble, whatever things are just, whatever things are pure, whatever things are lovely, whatever things are of good report, if there is any virtue and if there is anything praiseworthy—meditate on these things. The things which you learned and received and heard and saw in me, these do, and the God of peace will be with you" (Phil. 4:8–9).

More than that, we are commanded to give thanks in and for everything: "See that no one renders evil for evil to anyone, but always pursue what is good both for yourselves and for all. Rejoice always, pray without ceasing, in everything give thanks; for this is the will of God in Christ Jesus for you" (1 Thess. 5:15–18).

The answer to this curious mystery lies in the fact that we—the redeemed of God—have been and are being rescued from the former world of sin and misery. We have begun that process, here and now, whereby we will indeed arrive at our final destination, a place free of sin and misery. While we are not waiting for pie in the sky by and by, we have actually already begun receiving the benefits of redemption. Paul calls us to give "thanks to the Father who has qualified us to be partakers of the inheritance of the saints in the light. He has delivered us from the power of darkness and conveyed us into the kingdom of the Son of His love, in whom we have redemption through His blood, the forgiveness of sins" (Col. 1:12–14).

This new life is set in contrast with the old:

> Therefore be imitators of God as dear children. And walk in love, as Christ also has loved us and given Himself for us, an offering and a sacrifice to God for a sweet-smelling aroma. But fornication and all uncleanness or covetousness, let it not even be named among you, as is fitting for saints; neither filthiness, nor foolish talking, nor coarse jesting, which are not fitting, but rather giving of thanks (Eph. 5:1–4).

Even when we are troubled by the evil and the dreadful things of this world, we are exhorted to

> Rejoice in the Lord always. Again I will say, rejoice! Let your gentleness be known to all men. The Lord is at hand. Be anxious for nothing, but in everything by prayer and supplication, with thanksgiving, let your requests be made known to God; and the peace of God, which surpasses all understanding, will guard your hearts and minds through Christ Jesus (Phil. 4:4–7).

As we come to our loaded boards and behold the sights and aromas and tastes and textures of God's goodness, we should see with new eyes that God has indeed prepared a Table for us in the presence of our enemies. It is one more token of redemption begun. It is the appetizer before the eternal marriage feast of the Lamb. Let us give thanks!

*The Lord's Table and Our Tables*

At the Lord's Table, if we each just came in and picked up some bread and wine when it suited us and then consumed it privately, we would not be discerning the Lord's Body and we would not be joining in communion. We would be missing the point. The Table is the meeting place where we remember who we are and what has been done for us. We remember that we are dependent and that God is our Provider. We remember that we are not our own but belong to Christ and are members of one another. We enter into fellowship with God as He serves us and with one another as we share this meal. We are nourished and renewed at this Table. We leave this Table, therefore, ready to live in the context of all those lessons.

Similar things should be taught and received at our daily family tables, but this Great Table is where we start. It is here where things are set right and our lives as Christians are brought into their proper focus. The meal is simple, but the lessons are large. Let us eat this covenant meal and renew our covenant oath of loyalty to our Triune God.

We must start thinking about our family tables as little versions of the Lord's Table. We are still His people when we leave here. Having practiced the liturgy, we leave to live it. Too many families have abandoned or neglected the family table. Between fast-food, drive-thrus, and TV, few families sit down and eat together, much less do we self-consciously develop the table as a place of communion. We must gather around our individual family tables to commune with God and with one another. The parallels are powerful and important. As Robert Farrar Capon puts it, "The Table defines both the room it occupies and the household that gathers around it. It is the other first investment [the bed being the other—RB], and as long as the household lasts, it remains the one thing that everybody uses most—the one and often the only place where the family meets in fact."[2]

The table is to be a picture of hospitality, provision, and peace, but it's not automatic. Like the Lord's Table, the family table has to become a place where things happen. Capon continues about the table:

> Think of it first as a *thing*. To begin with, it is matter, not thought; it is not with us as the living-room furniture is with us—because we think it's a good idea; but with us as the bed is with us—because we cannot function without it. The poorest house has a table, and is by that very thing not so poor after all. But because it is a thing, because it is true to itself, it comes to us as things always come: raw, intractable, and unfinished. Planks on packing crates, or polished mahogany on delicate turnings, it is only itself. It will not turn from table into Board on its own motion any more than box spring and mattress will become marriage Bed without

---

[2] Robert Farrar Capon, *Bed and Board: Plain Talk About Marriage* (New York: Simon & Schuster, 1965), 93.

considerable care. It is there, and it is suitable, but the household that gathers around it must work to bring it into the dance. The table enters the exchanges of the family exactly as the stage enters into the ballet: as a thing, as itself, by being faithful to its own mute and stubborn materiality. It is the floor that makes possible the marvelous leap of grace; it is also the floor that punishes the less than marvelous one with disgrace. The table can make us or break us. It has its own laws and will not change. Food and litter will lie upon it; fair speech and venom will pour across it; it will be the scene of manners or meanness, the place of charity or the wall of division, depending. Depending on what is done with it, at it, and about it. But whatever is done, however it enters, it will allow only the possible, not the ideal. No one has ever created the Board by fiat. God himself spread his table, but Judas sat down at it. There is no use thinking that all we have to do is wish for a certain style of family life, and wait for it to happen. The Board is a union of thing and persons; what it becomes depends on how the thing is dealt with by the persons.[3]

There is one result, however, which will be produced automatically: The Board will always give birth to *liturgy*. Habits of form and order develop, consciously or unconsciously, at our tables, and these forms inevitably shape how we live. They will either be haphazard or else they will be full of meaning and purpose, but it is an inescapable concept that our table liturgy both reflects and directs who we are

---

[3] Capon, *Bed and Board*, 93–94.

and who we will become.

Furthermore, like the Lord our Shepherd in Psalm 23, we too should prepare our tables in the presence of our enemies. Life is full of enemies, including our own sinfulness, but the table is a place of victory and peace. It is a place of nourishment and encouragement. It is always a reminder of God's goodness to us.

I realized, as I was teaching a series on childrearing, that the family table is the place where it all comes together. We wash before we come to the table. Here, we are served and we have the opportunity to serve. We have rules and instruction to govern us (take off your hat).We have discipline (don't kick your sister; go to your room until you can act right, and so on).We have communion and fellowship. It is a place of thanksgiving and gratitude. It is a place of love. The table should cause us to pause regularly and re-focus on the importance of our Christian households.

*Ultimate Redemption of All Things*

When God first created the world, God gave the creation to Adam as food: "I have given you every plant yielding seed that is on the face of all the earth, and every tree which has fruit yielding seed; it shall be food for you" (Gen. 1:29). Adam was invited to the great banquet of creation so that he could eat and drink and rejoice in his God. All creation was a means for enjoying fellowship with the Creator.

That is the final destiny of the creation as well. In the renewed heavens and earth of the consummation, we will enjoy the marriage supper of the Lamb, the supper of the kingdom, forever. Many will come from the east and west to recline with Abraham, Isaac, Jacob, and Jesus in the kingdom.

And we are already enjoying that feast now; in this old creation, we are celebrating the feast of the new creation. With the bread and wine of the old world, we are anticipating the feast of the resurrection world. Even now in these decaying bodies we feed on the body and blood of Jesus. The Lord's Table points to the consummation of all things. Every week, the world of the future becomes present. At this meal the fruits of the earth, "the grain and new wine and oil," are made into the food of communion.

The bread and wine of this Table point to the destiny of all created things. It anticipates the time for which the creation eagerly waits, the time when creation will be set free of its slavery to corruption into the glorious freedom of the sons of God. From here, we are sent to our homes to repeat these lessons—to live them, connecting our worship to the way we live with one another.

There, at our little tables, we apply what we learn at the Great Table of the Lord.

## Conclusion

We gather again and again around our tables—small societies of Christians—learning to commune and share, to pray and talk, to receive and give thanks, to serve and be served, to love one another, and be renewed. We cannot neglect such an important huddle without the fragmentation of our little societies. Develop it, guard it, and practice it often.

# Chapter 5
# Missional Parenting
*Rich Lusk*

Build houses and live in them; plant gardens and eat their produce. Take wives and have sons and daughters; take wives for your sons, and give your daughters in marriage, that they may bear sons and daughters; multiply there, and do not decrease. But seek the welfare of the city where I have sent you into exile, and pray to the Lord on its behalf, for in its welfare you will find your welfare (Jer. 29:5–7)

The Lord said, "Shall I hide from Abraham what I am about to do, seeing that Abraham shall surely become a great and mighty nation, and all the nations of the earth shall be blessed in him? For I have chosen him, that he may command his children and his household after him to keep the way of the Lord by doing righteousness and justice, so that the Lord may bring to Abraham what he has promised him" (Gen. 18:17–19)

## Jeremiah 29:4-7: Raising Children in Exile

God has called parents into a great and glorious mission. Indeed, Christian parenting is a vital part of the Church's overarching mission of bringing blessing to the nations (Gen. 12:1-3; Matt. 28:16-20).

What is missional parenting? Jeremiah 29 helps explain. The book of Jeremiah is a letter from the prophet Jeremiah to the Jewish exiles who have been carted off to Babylon. In light of the sustained unfaithfulness of the nation, God has finally brought judgment against them. They are now dwelling among pagan peoples in a pagan city. They need to know: "What do we do here now that we are dwelling among pagans?" Jeremiah writes a letter to them, giving counsel and instruction, recorded for us in Jeremiah 29:4–32.

This passage is extremely appropriate for God's people today because the Church in our culture has entered into something of an exilic situation. If you are familiar with the history of Western Civilization, you know that, whatever its flaws, it was largely built on the backs of Bible-believing and Christ-trusting people. Now, all that seems to be crumbling; a once strong Christian consensus has evaporated all around us. We can despair over that. But when the dust clears, we have to ask, "What do we do *now*?" Jeremiah's letter teaches us how to live as pilgrims in a strange land. Geographically, we have not moved or been displaced, but culturally we have most certainly entered a period of exile for the Church.

What does Jeremiah say to the exiles dwelling in Babylon? He tells them to settle down, build houses, plant gardens, and have children. He tells them to seek after and pray for the peace (*shalom*) of the city. Why would

Jeremiah need to command them to have children in exile? How would having children play into their peace-seeking mission? Some of them may have thought that it would be better not to have kids while living in Babylon. False prophets had told them exile would never happen, or if it did, it wouldn't last long. Jeremiah knows it will last more than a generation and has told them so. He wanted them to think about the exile in multi-generational terms. We must do the same. Our culture in general and cities in particular may not appear like hospitable places for raising children, but part of seeking the *shalom* of Babylon is begetting sons and daughters. Why is this? Because one of the ways we seek to bless the city is through godly, faithful family life. There is a real temptation for us to be escapists and to sequester ourselves in little Christian enclaves, but Jeremiah calls us to engage the city, *including how we raise our children.*

But how do we raise up a godly generation in exile, in a culture with radically different values than our own? The Israelites would have asked that question; we need to ask it as well. In fact, we might wish that Jeremiah had sent along more detailed instructions about raising kids in Babylon. If he had said, "Hey parents, this is how much Babylonian TV your kids can watch each week. This is a list of approved Babylonian radio stations. Here's what you should do about the Babylonian city schools," it would have been very helpful. Jeremiah did not do that, of course, but that doesn't mean that we are left in the dark. Rather, it means we have to fill in Jeremiah's command using wisdom drawn from the rest of Scripture.

Interestingly, Paul is doing the same thing in Ephesians 6:4 when he gives instructions to parents seeking to raise up a godly generation in the midst of another pagan city, the city of Ephesus. Paul commands, "Fathers, raise up your children in the training and admonition of the Lord." The word for training in Greek is *paideia*. It is an all-encompassing term which essentially means our children are to be socialized into the life and culture of the kingdom of God. It's as though Paul says to them, "You may be citizens of the Roman Empire, but raise your children to live as citizens of God's kingdom. You must teach them what it means to live as Christians in a non-Christian environment."

When we get into the specifics of raising children in an ungodly milieu, there is no way we can take a one-size-fits-all approach that will answer every question for every family. But what I want to do here is sketch out an over-arching vision from which we can derive practical guidelines. Most importantly, we want to answer the question, "How does raising children fit into this mission Jeremiah gives to the Church of seeking the peace of the city?"

## Genesis 18:16–19:
## Raising Children to Bless the World

Modern churches spend a lot of time trying to develop mission statements. Abraham got his mission statement directly from God (Gen. 12:1–3). Abraham's mission would be to bring the blessing of God to all the nations of the world. He was chosen not just for his own benefit, but to be an agent of blessing to others. Abraham is blessed to be a blessing. Now, in Genesis 18, God reiterates that purpose, but explains further how Abraham's family will be instrumental in the fulfillment of his mission.

What was the blessing God bestowed on Abraham? According to the book of Galatians, it was the forgiveness of sins and the gift of the Holy Spirit. In other words, the blessing is the gospel! It is God's grace to us and our children. However, it is all too easy for us to focus on the first part of the Abrahamic covenant (God blessing us) and ignore the second part (our calling to bless others). It is also easy for us to ignore the role of descendants in our calling to be a blessing to others. If God has blessed our families with salvation, he wants us to be instruments of blessing others with salvation as well.

How will God's purpose of blessing the nations through Abraham come to pass? A careful look at the grammar of Genesis 18:19 yields an answer and helps us put the task of parenting in its proper place. There are three clauses in this verse that are joined together by two "in order that" statements. These statements unfold a logical progression. Abraham is chosen *in order that* he might command his family to walk in the way of the Lord *in order that* the promises made to him that all the families of the earth will be blessed will come to fulfillment. He is chosen to teach his family so that through his family all the nations of the earth will be blessed. Note that family life is not an end in itself; the family serves the larger mission of God's kingdom. Parenting is a second order task, subordinate to the fulfillment of Abraham's "Great Commission" of blessing the nations.

To make this more explicit, consider the structure of Genesis 18:19 more carefully:

(1) Abraham is chosen
> *in order that*
>> (2) he may train his children in justice and righteousness
>>> *in order that*
>>>> (3) the promise of global blessing may be fulfilled.

The problem is that many Christian parents get stuck on the middle term, (2), in the logical flow. We raise moral children as an end in itself, but we do not reach the ultimate missional goal of raising children who can reach the world with the blessing of the gospel. Parents and pastors alike simply must get this: *We should not aim at familiocentric churches, but at ecclesiocentric families.* Raising children rightly is simply a stepping stone; it's penultimate. The real goal is to plug our children into the mission of the Church.

Of course, missional families will grow and thrive only when they are joined together in missional churches. It is all too easy for churches to become ingrown and inward facing, only servicing the needs of their niche membership. It has been rightly said, "The Church exists for the sake of the world." So what are we doing to make our churches places where sinners can find Jesus? Where less mature Christians can find proper instruction and nourishment? If our church life and culture are set up only to accommodate people who have attained a high level of Christian maturity, we are actually failing; true maturity is found in sacrificial mission. A couple of (rather controversial) examples may help prove the point.

Should a church have a staffed nursery during the worship service? A pragmatic argument could be made in favor of a nursery even for mature Christian families who are working hard at training their children to stay in the whole worship service. Inevitably, there are times when moms have to take their little ones out. A nursery can actually maximize the number of people in the service by coordinating child care. Instead of five moms each individually taking their babies out, a nursery allows two moms (or other volunteers) to watch all five children.

But more importantly, there are missional reasons for having a staffed nursery. It is a function of congregational hospitality to the outsider. The reality is, most non-Christian families will not be able to keep small children with them in the whole service without too much of a struggle. Even most Christian parents today have simply not been given the resources or vision they need to train their children to stay in the service and learn to worship with the rest of the body. If our churches are not going to be only for those who have "arrived," then we need to be willing to accommodate folks while we work to get them up to speed. This is *not* compromise; rather, it's a form of congregational hospitality.

The problem is especially acute with non-Christian families who visit our churches. If we want them to be able to explore the Christian faith with us, they have to hang around long enough to hear what we have to say and get to know us. But that simply cannot happen if we are not prepared to shoulder the burden of some of their child care needs on Sundays. Having a nursery for the little ones is a way we can meet people where they are, and then help play catch up.

For the same reasons, we need Sunday School or something very much like it. To be sure, I think a strong case can be made for age-segregated Sunday School classes as a common sense way to supplement parental instruction that is already taking place. It is good and healthy for our children to learn from other members of the body of Christ besides their parents (though parents should be warned of the dangers of abdicating as well). But more to the point, there are missional reasons for having a Sunday School program. Sunday School was originally started in the eighteenth century as an outreach program to illiterate children, to teach them to read through teaching them the Bible. Some have used Sunday School's origins as a reason to discontinue it, but I see its origins as a strong incentive for keeping it around (or developing something similar to the traditional Sunday School program in its place). Sunday School is not just for the insider, but also for the outsider; it's not just for furthering discipleship, but for doing evangelism.

Consider the following scenario: Someone in your church befriends a single mom with two boys, ages nine and eleven, and invites her to church. Her boys are in a below average public school. They were baptized as babies, but have never been in church regularly. They have not had much instruction and are quite a handful. The mom is starting to really lose control, and the window of opportunity to set the boys on a good life path is rapidly closing. What does the church have to offer her and her children? It would be great if we could press the "pause" button on the boys, get her up to speed, and then let her resume her work of parenting. But that can't happen. She's going to have to learn on the "go" how to handle her children. But in the meantime they continue to grow up. So how can the church best help her?

Certainly families should have her family into their homes and develop strong relationships with her and her children. Men in the church should help provide a masculine presence in their lives. But the church can also speed up the process by providing direct instruction to her boys. One of the best things the church can offer her boys is consistent teaching in the form of a Sunday School program (or something like it). As the boys are taught truth, they also get to be around other kids who are already on track, so they have mature peer group examples all around them. Sunday School is not the only solution to the scenario I've described, but it can be a vital piece of it. Unless our churches are only going to cater to intact, traditional families, to the exclusion of almost everyone else, we need to develop ways of ministering to people from broken backgrounds. Familiocentric churches do a good job keeping the "healthy" well, but they simply cannot minister to the "sick" very effectively. Missional churches and families aim to find ways to befriend sinners where they are, not where they should have been. Only in this way can we be the blessing God promised through Abraham.

## Genesis 18:16–19:
## A Missional Curriculum for Parents

The family exists for the sake of the Church, and the Church exists for the sake of the world. So how can parents train their children to play their part in the global mission of the Church? Unpacking Genesis 18:19 further, in what specifically is Abraham to train his children? He is to train them in the way of the Lord: to do righteousness and justice. God tells Abraham to teach his children, and then God gives him the curriculum. "Keeping the way of the Lord" or "walking in the way of the Lord" is a common Old Testament expression for the pattern of life that God calls His people to embody. To walk in the way of the Lord means walking in the way of the Lord and *not* in the way of some other god or idol. It means not walking according to your own light, but according to the light of God's Word. Walking in the way of the Lord also means imitating God; it means observing how God acts, and then modeling your conduct, your lifestyle, and your relationships after His. Parents are to teach their children to live a God-like lifestyle.

Another way to unpack what it means to walk in the way of the Lord is to look to God's law. To walk in the way of the Lord is to do the things that God has specifically commanded and instructed us to do in His Word, knowing that any other path we might try to follow is a dead end. The pathway marked out for us in the law of God is the one and only path that leads to life. Walking in the way of the Lord is a matter of keeping His commandments because His laws reflect His character and action (e.g., Deut. 10:17–19). Thus, parents are to teach their children to adhere to God's Word in all of life.

The content of this missional curriculum is spelled out further with the words "righteousness" and "justice." These are two closely related terms, though they have slightly different shades of meaning. "Righteousness" refers to something that is what it should be, something that fulfills its design or meets its standards or satisfies its purpose. It is a relational and covenantal term. A righteous person is the person who keeps his word and fulfills his obligations to others; he is what a human being should be in his community. He does right by others because he lives in his relationships according to God's design. He is covenantally faithful. In a fallen world, righteousness means not only doing what is right, but right-wising what is wrong; it means working to put the world to rights. Thus, relational righteousness ultimately means restoring broken people to health, safety, and prosperity; it means bringing people into the *shalom* God intended for the creation from the beginning.

Justice is closely related to righteousness. Justice is the action of setting things right; it is righting wrongs. When things are out of order, justice puts them back in order. When things are out of place, justice puts them back in their place. Where things are broken, justice fixes them. Biblical justice is not just confined to the law court. Justice is not only a judge's declaration, but the follow-through, the execution of the sentence. Moreover, while biblical justice is multifaceted, so that acting in justice varies according to one's role and circumstances, justice in the Bible always carries not only a punitive dimension, but a restorative dimension as well. This is why justice in the Bible is so often closely related to mercy, peace, and compassion (e.g., Zech. 7:9–10; Job 29:12–17). Whether it is caring for the poor or rescuing the oppressed or acting on behalf of those who cannot act for themselves, it is an act of mercy from one perspective, but from another perspective, it is an act of justice. Justice is giving others what God says we owe them, which, of course, is love above all else.

It is crucial to understand that in the Old Testament righteousness and justice are not concepts or doctrines we are to think about, but rather are things we do and practice in the world. And when we *do* righteousness and justice, the result is blessing and *shalom*. Thus, the mission of Genesis 12 and Jeremiah 29 of bringing blessing to the nations and *shalom* to the city, is fulfilled when God's people do righteousness and justice. What is God telling Abraham in Genesis 18:19? He is telling him to teach his children to obey and imitate God, to pursue righteousness and justice, and in this way bring about restoration, healing, blessing, and peace in the world. As N. T. Wright puts it:

> To hope for a better future in this world—for the poor, the sick, the lonely and depressed, for the slaves, the refugees, the hungry and homeless, for the abused, the paranoid, the downtrodden and despairing, and in fact for the whole wide, wonderful and wounded world—is not something else, something extra, something tacked on to the gospel as an afterthought.[1]

The practice of righteousness and justice is integral to a gospel-shaped life.

Where does the preaching of the gospel fit into this ministry of righteousness and justice? Obviously, preaching the gospel is indispensable to bringing blessing and peace to the city. Only the gospel can deal with the root of the world's fallenness and give hurting people victory over the last enemy of death. But word and deed ministry go together. They did in the life of Jesus (Luke 24:19), and they continue to in the life of the Church (Rom. 15:18; 1

---

[1] N. T. Wright, *Surprised by Hope: Rethinking Heaven, the Resurrection, and the Mission of the Church* (New York: Harper, 2008), 192–193.

Pet. 4:11). Jesus got a hearing from His contemporaries because of what He was doing. They saw Him saving people from sickness and death, and so they listened when He talked about salvation and forgiveness. The Church is now to embody the same pattern. We must not fall into a false dichotomy between evangelism and social action. Both are mandatory for the body of Christ because both are part of our holistic mission of justice and righteousness.

## Missional Parenting

We tend to think of mission and parenting as standing in sharp tension with one another. Mission has to do with reaching the world, interacting with and engaging unbelievers. Mission has to do with facing the challenges and temptations that come with engaging the culture. Mission is what we do out in the world; it is outward-facing. Parenting, on the other hand, has to do with nurturing and protecting children. It has to do with shielding children from the world's evil, at least until they are mature enough to deal with it. Parenting seems to be inward-facing. Thus, there seems to be a tension between the task of mission and the task of parenting.

Churches seem to swing one way or the other. Some churches have a strong focus on missions, but usually end up neglecting their own children. Other churches focus so heavily on nurturing their own children that they ignore those on the outside. The Church is just there to meet family needs and only grows with nine months notice. It is more like a family club than a people sent on a global mission.

Genesis 18:19 will not allow us to go to either end of the spectrum because it requires us to do both. Mission and covenant succession go together, and to have one without the other is always disastrous for the Church. What good does it do if we reach the world but lose our children to the world in the process? What good does it do to reach people out there if we lose the children in here? If we are losing our own children to the world, we are never going to fulfill our mission. At the same time, what good does it do to raise up kids who are moral, but who are so separated from the world that they cannot carry the mission of the Church forward or engage the world around them? We are called to be different from the world for sure, but there are also ways in which we are called to be similar to the world around us. This is what the prophet Jeremiah is emphasizing when he speaks of living and participating in the city. Some Christians are too worldly, to be sure, but other Christians are not worldly enough in the right way.

One of the earliest pieces of Christian apologetics preserved from the ancient church, the "Letter to Diognetus," is very helpful in this regard. The letter is famous for developing its doctrine of dual citizenship. We are citizens of God's kingdom, but we are also citizens of an earthly society. We have an earthly citizenship and a heavenly citizenship, and we must live out both faithfully. Certainly, our heavenly citizenship controls the way we live out our earthly citizenship. The heavenly citizenship obviously has a higher rank. But some Christians have so separated themselves from the world around them that they are really not earthly citizens any longer, at least in any functional way. They are really not participating in the life of the culture around them, making it impossible for them to truly seek the peace of their city. Yes, we are citizens of the kingdom of heaven, and that means we live out a distinctive lifestyle, but we are also citizens on earth. We are called to live out a form of life that shares all kinds of cultural space and all kinds of cultural traits with the people around us. This is crucial if we are to establish the points of contact necessary to move the mission forward (1 Cor. 9:19–23).

All that to say: There is a vital link between raising children and the mission of the Church, and this means parenting must have a missional flavor. Parenting is not an end in itself. Parenting is an "in order that" kind of thing, as Genesis 18:19 indicates. You don't just raise godly children so you'll have godly children. You raise godly children so they can carry forth the mission that God entrusted to Abraham in the beginning, a mission that God reiterated to the exiles through Jeremiah. True Christian parenting aims at producing children who are a blessing, who bring *shalom*. We seek to raise up a godly generation not for its own sake, but for the sake of the city and for the sake of the world. Parental nurture feeds and supports kingdom mission.

This means there is something bigger at stake in your parenting than having a happy family life. Moreover, it means parenting is more complicated than just saying "no" to the things of the world. We must be *missional parents*, raising *missional children*. Again, faithful parenting isn't just a matter of building a hedge around the home to keep pop culture out. Sure, parents need to protect and shelter their children in appropriate ways; we don't just throw our children into the world, for that would be like throwing them to the wolves. However, neither can we settle for raising them to live in a Christian ghetto or evangelical subculture. We raise them up so they can play their part and participate in this mission in the world. We raise them to be savvy about culture and winsome in how they present the gospel. If all you do is seek to protect your children, your parental endeavors are terribly incomplete. Parents are not engaged in a rear guard, defensive action. Genesis 18:19 calls us to offensive, missionally aggressive parenting.

Psalm 127 talks about our children as a quiver full of arrows. It does no good to sharpen and straighten those arrows if you are just going to leave them in the quiver. We have to string our bows and unleash our children into the world, firing them into the heart of enemy territory. Our children have to learn how to live in the world the same way a doctor has to learn to work around sick people without contracting illness. Our children have to be prepared to go into the world the same way a doctor has to go into the sick ward, for only then can they bring the healing power of the gospel to bear on the brokenness of the world. Too many of us are in danger of ending up with finely honed, sharpened, straightened arrows that never get drawn out of the quiver; too many of us are in danger of raising knowledgeable "doctors" who never cure anyone because they're afraid to enter the hospital. Our children cannot bless the world if they never go out into the world. They cannot seek the peace of the city unless they engage the culture and people of the city. We are to train our children not just to avoid evil, but to conquer evil. We are to train children who know, not just how to interpret the world, but how to transform it.

## Kids to the Rescue

The story of Sodom and Gomorrah is odd because, while it comes in the context of the life of Abraham, it seems to work at cross-purposes with God's promises to Abraham. God has promised Abraham global blessing, but

Genesis 18 and 19 are about judgment. Instead of sharing in the blessing of God, wrath falls from heaven on the cities of the plain.

What initially attracts the Lord's attention to Sodom is not its wickedness but the great outcry that rises up from the city (Gen. 18:20–21). The word for "outcry" describes a cry for help, a cry for deliverance from oppression, cruelty, violence, and tyranny. It is the same word used later to describe the cry of the Israelites in slavery in Egypt. In Deuteronomy 22, the same word is used to describe a woman's cry for help when she is being raped. The word "outcry" reminds us that Sodom was a brutal place, full of both sexual and social perversity (cf. Ezek. 16:48–49).

But why can't Sodom be saved? Why can't Sodom be rescued at this point in time? The reason even Abraham's prayers cannot save the city is because Abraham does not yet have a family. God tells Abraham he is to raise children to do righteousness and justice, and He tells him that in the midst of going to investigate and then destroy unrighteous and unjust cities. How do these things fit together? Why does the Lord stop to speak to Abraham about his future family while going to judge the unjust cities? The answer is simple: Abraham's offspring will be the answer to Sodom's problems. God has chosen Abraham so that he can raise up children who will do justice and righteousness *and in this way* answer the outcry of Sodom-like cities in the future. When the Lord blesses him with a family, Abraham must raise up his children in the way of the Lord so they can answer the city's cry for help and bring justice and blessing to the Sodoms of the world. The justice and righteousness of Abraham's children will meet and overcome the injustice and unrighteousness of the city, conquering curse with blessing and violence with *shalom*.

Abraham cannot rescue the city at this point in history because he doesn't yet have a family. But in the future, the task of the sons of Abraham will be to serve as the righteous in the city who bring blessing and save the city from judgment. As members of the Abrahamic covenant, this is the job of Christian parents today: We are to raise up children who can save our cities, who can rescue our modern day Sodoms by bringing the blessing and *shalom* of the gospel to them. Abraham longed to see the city saved; we must have that same longing. However, Abraham lacked the necessary instrument, namely, children. We do not. Our children must grow to be the "Restorer of Streets to Dwell In" (Isa. 58:12), bringing the dead streets of our cities to life through gospel messaging and gospel neighboring, through gospel proclamation and gospel embodiment.

## Kingdom Kids, Church Kids, Apostolic Kids

Think about what Jesus said concerning covenant children in Matthew 19:14: "Let the little children come to me, and do not forbid them; for of such is the kingdom of heaven" (NKJV). While this passage is one of those texts that gets all tied up in debates over paedobaptism and paedocommunion, we should not miss the missional implications.

Jesus says the kingdom belongs to our children and our children belong to the kingdom. Certainly, Jesus is teaching that the privileges and benefits of the kingdom belong to our children. But if they have been blessed with kingdom life, they must learn to be a blessing to others. If the kingdom belongs to them, the mission of the kingdom belongs to them as well. Kingdom membership is not just about privileges; it carries with it responsibilities. Our children are part of the family of Abraham, called to be *shalom* seekers for the world around them.

Raising kingdom kids means a lot more than just raising kids who are "good Christians" and stay out of trouble. It means more than teaching kids to pray and stay chaste. It means that we as parents cannot allow our kids to settle for a privatized righteousness. We cannot settle for moral kids; we must raise missional kids, kids who learn to live with a sense of being "sent" into the world with a divine mandate. This means raising children is a form of missionary training.

In Ephesians 6, Paul tells fathers to bring their children up "in the nurture and admonition of the Lord" (KJV). This includes training them to look at the world through the lens of God's mission. Thus, parents must inculcate a heart for mission in their children. Paul also gives children the command to honor their parents (Eph. 6:1–3). Given that Paul has addressed his letter to the church in Ephesus (Eph. 1:1ff.), and now addresses the children as a subgroup within the church, it is safe to say that our children should be considered members of the "one, holy, catholic, and apostolic church."

What does it mean for the Church to be "apostolic"? An apostle is one who is sent. "Apostolic" basically means "missional"; the two words are essentially interchangeable. (Some folks don't like the word "missional" because it has become too much of a trendy buzz word; if that's the case, I suggest using the term "apostolic" instead.) To be missional is to be apostolic and vice versa. We are sent on a mission; all Christians are apostles in a broad sense. Our children are sent on a mission as apostles as well. This mission, this "sent-ness," has to flavor, contextualize, and shape everything that we do. We live as God's sent people no matter what we are doing at any given moment. We are bearers of the kingdom of God and representatives of God's righteousness and justice in everything that we do. We are called to bring *shalom* into the world as we obey God in all of life through the generations.

So where do we begin? Parents, the best way to train your kids in *shalom*-making is to do it yourself. You have to be the kind of person you want your children to become. You have to model missional blessing in your own life.

This is precisely what Abraham goes on to do in Genesis 18 when he intercedes for Sodom and Gomorrah. Abraham prays for the cities of the plain, seeking their rescue, blessing, and salvation. He knows the Lord is going to inspect them and will eventually judge them. But he does not just pull up a lawn chair to watch the fireworks show. He does not cheer on the wrath from heaven (unlike the prophet Jonah, later in history, when he wished destruction on Nineveh). Instead, he seeks to protect and shield the cities through his prayers. Abraham acts like and prays like a missionary, setting an example for us and for our children. He is a missional man living out the mission, seeking the good of the place where God has put him. Do we teach our children to pray missionally? Or do their prayers fixate on personal and familial needs? It's great to pray for grandma's health or a safe trip on the family vacation, but our children need to learn how to use prayer as more than a means of seeking their personal and familial well-being. We must equip them to use prayer as a tool for seeking blessing and *shalom* for the broken world around them, including "the least of these."

Just as mission became a core part of Abraham's identity, so it must become a core part of our identity and our children's identity. Parents, it is your job to set before your children an example of justice and righteousness and to knead these things into the hearts of your children. In light of these imperatives, a couple of suggestions are in order.

First, parents must do more than fill their children up with doctrine and good teaching; they must fill them up with love and affection to the point of overflowing, as well. When children are loved affectionately, they have a surplus they can share with others. Kids who have a love deficiency don't make very good missionaries because they have no love to share. So love your kids deeply and consistently. This includes not only teaching and discipline, but also much, much more. The missional home is a home filled with love and joy; it is a place permeated with an atmosphere of mutual service and encouragement.

Second, parents must make outbound mission a way of life for the whole family. Go find people in need! Invite others into your home and teach your children how to be hosts. Don't merely invite social peers; invite the poor, the lonely, and the needy. Invite single moms into your home. Invite families on your street who do not share your way of life, political views, educational choices, and so on. Invite outsiders in and love them with the love of Christ. Make your home a place of mercy and hospitality and missional prayer. Make your home an outpost of the kingdom and a launching pad for gospel outreach.

You might say, "Well, that's taking the focus off my kids. I might end up neglecting my kids if I try to do all that." The reality is that children thrive when they grow up in a home where the parents are constantly seeking to expand their range of service for the kingdom. They see what kingdom life looks like from the inside. They have their natural sense of selfishness subverted. If we do this right, our children will not see this as an alternative to spending time with them ("Oh, Mom and Dad are doing hospitality instead of being with me"); rather, they will see themselves as vital participants in a family ministry ("This is something we as a family do to care for others and share our blessings"). Make your family a home base of mercy, justice, righteousness, and blessing in the world.

If we just give our children doctrine and morality without a gospel-driven love for the lost and poor, we are actually raising up a new generation of Pharisees. We must raise children who can reach out to the different and difficult, with the grace and mercy of Christ. We need to train our children to keep their spiritual antenna up so they can pick up distress signals being sent out all around them. In this way, they can learn to be agents of blessing and peace in the world so that all God promised to Abraham and commanded through Jeremiah will come to pass. Our families have been blessed with the love and forgiveness of Christ; now it is time to go bless others with the same.

# Chapter 6
# What Is Marriage For?
*Rich Lusk*

Getting married is dangerous. When you get married, you do not know what the future holds. You do not know how your new spouse might change. You do not know what sicknesses they might contract or into what sins they might fall. Marriage is intrinsically risky. It is all the more dangerous in our culture because marriage as an institution is under attack in our day. While we might expect liberals to attack marriage, what is surprising and disappointing is the inability of conservatives—including conservative Christians—to defend marriage as an institution.

A recent *Newsweek* article entitled, "Marriage Is Hard: The Religious Right Admits It," shows the problem.[1] The article chronicles the recent marital failures of several high-profile conservative evangelicals, like Senator John Ensign, who was known as a "family values" Republican. Ensign voted to impeach Bill Clinton in 2004 because of his misconduct and was known for strongly supporting a constitutional amendment defending the institution of marriage. Senator Ensign wrote, "Marriage is an extremely

---

[1] Lisa Miller, "Marriage Is Hard: The Religious Right Admits It," *Newsweek* 154.16 (Oct. 8, 2009): 25. Online: http://www.thedailybeast.com/newsweek/2009/10/07/marriage-is-hard.html.

important institution in this country and protecting it is, in my mind, worth the extraordinary step of amending our constitution." And yet apparently his own marriage was not worth guarding against adultery. The same *Newsweek* article suggested that the failure of so many high profile rightwing marriages have destroyed conservatives' credibility on the marriage question. What the political right *says* about marriage has no power because what they *do* looks so much like everyone else. In other words, their case for marriage is subverted by their hypocrisy in their own marriages.

Marriage is under attack, which means marriage must be defended. But in the Church it is vital for us to understand that whatever defense of marriage we offer has to be not only spoken but also embodied. The issue will not be won on the political battlefield, but in the bedrooms, kitchens, dining rooms, and family rooms of our homes. The best defense of marriage we can offer is . . . well, our own marriages. But for our marriages to defend marriage properly, they must be strong, healthy, beautiful, and biblically formed. We must guard and defend our own *particular* marriages if we are going to guard and defend the *institution* of marriage. If the Church is not known as a place where married life is practiced with holy joy and where spouses warmly cherish one another in lifelong fidelity, then nothing we say in defense of marriage will ever get any traction. Our public defense of marriage has to be wedded to (pun intended!) the practice of prizing marriage in our own homes.

We need to revisit the biblical foundations of marriage. The best place to begin is, of course, in the beginning with God's creation of marriage. We need to understand why God created marriage. What is the purpose of marriage anyway?

Let me begin by stating what the purpose of marriage is *not*. In many ancient and traditional societies, marriage was treated as a business proposition. People got married to further the family estate and to produce heirs who would carry on a family name. Marriage was a kind of business deal aimed at upgrading family status. Things like companionship and romance were not on the radar screen, at least not as they are today. Family honor, social status, and the economic well-being and protection of the extended family were paramount. This is why arranged marriages were so common: Mom and Dad could set up an advantageous marriage for the whole clan because marriage was driven largely by political and economic factors, not romantic factors.

Modern societies have taken a very different tack. Today, people marry (supposedly) for love. But love, biblically defined, is all about sacrifice, and modern people, being staunch individualists, are not very good at sacrifice. So it would be more honest to say that today people really marry for self-fulfillment even if it's dressed in the guise of love. What is marriage *for* in the modern world? It is *for me*. Why get married? Today, people get married to express themselves, to satisfy their desires, and because it *feels* good.

The problem with this is obvious: If you married for the sake of personal fulfillment, what do you do when someone else comes along who can provide greater fulfillment? Statistics and the sad wreckage of the modern American family life show us: People simply hop out of one relationship and into another. And it's fully justified because they're just following their heart... or whatever. But it has become very clear that in the modern world marriage is treated as a commodity. Premarital relationships are a way of shopping around to find the best deal. And when another potential partner comes along who looks like more of a bargain, we start "shopping" there instead.

Of course, it is also easy to see how this consumerist approach plays into things like homosexual marriage. If marriage is about self-fulfillment and gays are told they cannot marry, then we are blocking their pathway to fulfilled lives. The logic of our heterosexual unions and the modern habit of serial adultery via divorce and remarriage make homosexual marriages seem completely normal and natural.

But what does God have to say? What is marriage for, biblically speaking? God has something very different in mind for marriage. The biblical approach to marriage is not the marriage-as-business-deal arrangement of many pre-modern societies, but neither is it the marriage-as-self-actualization model we find in the modern world.

There are three clearly definable divine purposes in marriage.

First, according to the Scriptures, marriage is for the sake of gospel symbolism. Marriage is fundamentally a metaphor, an image of something beyond itself. In Ephesians 5, Paul says marriage "is a great mystery, but I speak concerning Christ and the Church" (v. 32 NKJV). It is not as if God created marriage and then afterwards said, "You know, this would actually make a pretty good picture of the relationship I have with my people." It is the other way around. God always intended to unite Himself to His people, to marry His people, and so He created human marriage to reveal and symbolize that plan. As husbands and wives live together in a biblical marriage, they signify and point to Christ and the Church, respectively. In Ephesians 5, Christ's marriage to the Church is presented as the foundation of human marriage. Our marriages are derivative and secondary. Our marriages are the copy; Christ and the Church are the original. The first thing you must understand about marriage is that marriage is not really *about* marriage; rather, marriage is about Christ and the Church. This symbolism is not added on top of marriage; it is the root and source of marriage. The greatness of marriage is found in what it symbolizes. The greatest privilege of marriage is getting to act out the gospel drama of Christ and the Church on a daily basis with the world looking on as an inquisitive audience.

While this symbolism obviously exalts marriage, this same symbolism also reminds us that marriage is not ultimate, but penultimate. The reality that marriage points to is greater than marriage itself. If you try to make marriage into something more than it is, your final source of fulfillment and meaning, you will crush yourself, your spouse, and your children. Marriage, like any good thing outside of God himself, can be turned into an idol if we want it too much or demand too much from it. Some people actually make marriage into an alternative gospel, a kind of substitute salvation. They think, "If only I could marry a person like A, B, or C, then I would be happy," or "If only my spouse would do X, Y, or Z, then I would be fulfilled." But this is a form of idolatry. The biggest problem with marriage in our circles is not indifference but idolatry. We need to understand that family life is not everything. We all too easily hurt most those we love most precisely because we are most likely to make idols of them, expecting them to provide us with a joy and security that no created thing can deliver. Ernest Becker put it well when he wrote, "No human relationship can bear the burden of godhood."[2] Alexander Schmemann is even more to the point:

> A marriage which does not constantly crucify its own selfishness and self-sufficiency, which does not "die to itself" that it may point beyond itself, is not a Christian marriage. The real sin of marriage today is not adultery or lack of "adjustment" or "mental cruelty." It is the idolization of the family itself, the refusal to understand marriage as directed toward the Kingdom of God. . . . It is not the lack of respect for the family, it is the idolization of the family that breaks the modern family so easily, making divorce its almost natural shadow. It is the identification of marriage with happiness and the refusal to accept the cross in it.[3]

Here is one way to test yourself whether you are gravitating toward this type of idolatry (familiolatry): What do you do when your spouse or children let you down? Do you get extremely angry and impatient? Do you have a hard time forgiving in such situations? If so, you need to be reminded that only the love of Christ for His Bride can really fulfill and satisfy you at the core of your being. You do not need your spouse to be your savior or your god because you already have a God and a Savior in Christ. Your marriage's fundamental purpose is to reveal to the world the Christ/Church relationship, not to make you happy all the time. Accept the cross in your marriage, and live ac-

---

[2] Ernest Becker, *The Denial of Death* (reprint, New York: Free Press, 1997), 166.

[3]     Alexander Schmemann, *For the Life of the World: Sacraments and Orthodoxy*, 2ⁿᵈ ed. (Crestwood, NY: St. Vladimir's Seminary Press, 1998), 90.

cordingly. The happiest marriages are not those that aim at marital happiness but that aim at the kingdom of God.

Second, God created marriage for the sake of companionship. Marriage is the most intense and complete form of friendship in the whole of creation. We all know the story: After Adam is created, God brings him the animals for naming, but Adam does not find a suitable helper among them. God then puts Adam into a death-like sleep and cuts him in two. When he awakens, he finds that God has made out of his side a bride, a wife. She is different from him, yet like him; mysteriously similar to him, but not identical to him. She is his perfect counterpart and the one in whom he finds completeness.

God said it was not good for Adam to be alone in the Garden. A bride was the one missing piece in an otherwise complete creation. The king needed his queen. Now Adam has his bride, and all is well. Adam has been reunited with his missing rib. This one flesh companionship is beautiful when lived out according to God's will and design. And, of course, this beautiful companionship ties back in to the symbolism of marriage.

To be sure, as we have seen, marriage is fundamentally symbolic, and in part what it symbolizes is the companionship of Christ and His Church. But biblical symbols in some way participate in the realities they represent. Thus, marital companionship is not just a matter of symbolism; it is also experience. Christian marriage not only reveals to the world God's covenantal relationship with His people, it is also for our well-being, as husbands and wives participate in the love of Christ by loving one another. Marriage is a joyous spiritual, social, and covenantal oneness with another person, with Christ himself as the glue that holds the two together in a one-flesh bond. Everything in marriage is shared; ultimately the husband and wife share life together in Christ. Christian marriage is the Edenic state recovered, where we are naked but not ashamed in the presence of God and one another. Marriage is a God-wrought, God-filled union between a man and a woman for His glory and the couple's good.

This is why all of our culture's attacks on marriage are so dangerous. They not only threaten the gospel symbolism God built into marriage; they also threaten the most fundamental fabric of human society. Marriage is foundational to any human society because it is the most basic, bedrock form of companionship there is. When the bonds of marital trust begin to fray on a wide scale, society as a whole begins to unravel.

The problem with premarital sex illustrates this. Premarital relations destroy our ability to have marital relations in a trusting way. Premarital relations create a kind of false oneness, a counterfeit of the oneness God intended. But this pseudo-oneness undercuts the genuine oneness of a biblical marriage, and thus of all true companionship.

Why does the Bible teach that sex outside of marriage is wrong? God does not ban premarital relations because He is a killjoy, but because He wants a greater joy for us, the joy of true oneness and holistic companionship. C. S. Lewis explains one reason why premarital sex is abominable: "The monstrosity of sexual intercourse outside marriage is that those who indulge in it are trying to isolate one kind of union (the sexual) from all the other kinds of union which were intended to go along with it and make up the total union."[4]

---

[4] C. S. Lewis, *Mere Christianity* (1952; reprint, New York: HarperCollins, 2001), 104–105.

What would you think about a man who opened up joint checking accounts with strange women he meets in bars? You'd say he's crazy! You cannot have economic oneness with women you hardly know and to whom you have no commitment. That kind of shared oneness belongs only within a covenantal, marital relationship. But if that's the case, how much more does the one flesh sexual union belong exclusively within the covenantal bond of marriage? The continual practice of partial oneness endangers and subverts the holistic oneness God desires for us.

Sometimes the companionship element of marriage is misunderstood. Our culture tends to sentimentalize it. We say things like, "If I can just find my soul mate, I will live happily ever after." But once we get married, we discover the reality of living together as one flesh requires a lot of hard work. To be frank, men and women are quite different from one another. While we are designed to complete one another, in a fallen world, this does not always happen the way it should because our masculinity and femininity are distorted by sin. The pieces of the marital puzzle do not always fit together as cleanly and perfectly as they should. Every marriage is going to have its quarrels; the key is to make sure they are lover's quarrels.

G.K. Chesterton once wrote, "Marriage is a duel to the death which no man of honour should decline."[5] In the 1930's, Chesterton observed that Americans had loosened their divorce laws, so that divorce for "reasons of incompatibility" was now legal. Chesterton quipped: "If Americans can be divorced for 'incompatibility of temper' I cannot conceive why they are not all divorced. I have known

---

[5] G. K. Chesterton, *Manalive* (1912; reprint, Harmondsworth, Middlesex, England: Penguin, 1947), 171.

many happy marriages, but never a compatible one."[6] The companionship dimension of marriage is not always easy, but the whole aim of marriage is to fight through those instances when incompatibility becomes unquestionable. When our incompatibilities bump up against each other, what do we do? Chesterton again helps us out of the jams by reminding us who we are as men and women:

> The differences between a man and a woman are at best so obstinate and exasperating that they practically cannot be got over unless there is an atmosphere of exaggerated tenderness and mutual interest. To put the matter in one metaphor, the sexes are two stubborn pieces of iron; if they are to be welded together, it must be while they are red-hot. Every woman has to find out that her husband is a selfish beast, because every man is a selfish beast by the standard of a woman. But let her find out the best while they are both still in the story of "Beauty and the Beast." Every man has to find out that his wife is cross—that is to say, sensitive to the point of madness; for every woman is mad by the masculine standard. But let him find out that she is mad while her madness is more worth considering than anyone else's sanity.[7]

Genesis 2 presents the complementarity of husband and wife in a beautiful way. When God brings Eve to

---

[6] G. K. Chesterton, *What's Wrong with the World?* (1910), in G. K. Chesterton, *The Collected Works of G. K. Chesterton*, vol. 4 (San Francisco: Ignatius, 1987), 70.

[7] G. K. Chesterton, "Two Stubborn Pieces of Iron," *The Common Man* (New York: Sheed & Ward, 1950), 142–143.

Adam in Genesis 2, Adam breaks out into song (the first love poetry in the Bible): "Bone of my bone and flesh of my flesh." Think about that imagery. Bone is hard, while flesh is soft. Adam is saying: "Where I am weak she will be strong, and where she is weak I will be strong, and together we will complete one another and become one. I am you and you are me, and together we are one flesh."

Admitting the struggles entailed in marital companionship opens the door to the third aspect of marriage: maturation, or transformation. God uses the marriage relationship to bring about the transformation of our character. In Ephesians 5:18–20, Paul describes the Spirit-filled life in musical terms: to be filled with the Spirit means singing and making music in your heart to the Lord. The Spiritual person is a musical person. The Spirit adds a musical quality to our lives. Just as song glorifies speech, so the presence of the Spirit elevates and beautifies everything in our lives. In verse 21, Paul begins unpacking various relationships in the Church, but there is no sharp change in subject. It is not as if Paul says, "Enough about this business of being filled with the Spirit! Now let's talk about family life." Paul is continuing to unfold what the Spiritual life looks like when he begins talking marriage, family, and work. The presence of the Spirit not only makes us musical in a literal sense, but the Spirit brings harmony to our relationships in a metaphorical sense as well. Just as the Spirit leads us to harmonize our voices in worship, so He leads us to harmonize together in family and social life. The absence of the Spirit means strife and bickering; the presence of the Spirit makes our relationships joyful, playful, and beautiful, like a well trained orchestra.

What does this "lived music" look like in the home? The Spirit makes our lives glorious and radiant by empowering us to fulfill our particular roles with charity and humility. The Christian marriage is a Spirit-filled song and dance; as with all dances, the man leads and the woman follows. Together their lives blend into one as they make the music of the Spirit.

How does the Spirit bring this about? Learning to dance well requires effort and discipline. It is interesting that historically the Church has treated celibacy as a kind of spiritual discipline; the chaste and faithful single life requires a special gift of the Spirit. But what is not widely recognized is that Christian marriage requires a special gift and work of the Spirit as well; like the Christian celibate, the Christian spouse needs to see his or her calling as both a Spiritual privilege and discipline. You must understand your marital life is an arena in which God will bring about the transformation of your character, exposing and remaking who you are. Let's consider some examples.

Marriage gives us new opportunities to learn the fine art of forgiveness. When your spouse sins against you, God is giving you an opportunity to show mercy and learn to forgive as you have been forgiven. Your spouse's failures are actually great for your transformation! Every time your spouse sins, you have a golden opportunity to grow Spiritually.

Marriage also teaches us humility by exposing our own sin. Marriage does not simply change who we are; it reveals who we are. Marriage is like a full length mirror for the heart. Marriage is a 24/7 relationship. It leaves you with no place to hide who you really are. Marriage exposes our selfishness, pride, impatience, and other assorted vices in a deeper way than any other human relationship. But, of course, each time sin is exposed, we have a new opportunity to repent and, therefore, to grow and mature as believers.

Marriage also teaches us wisdom. This happens in many ways, but consider: Men and women are different. Biblically, they are viewed as equals in creation and redemption, but they are not identical. These differences are notoriously difficult to articulate, so allow me to oversimplify. Men and women have different roles to play in the created order. Men are more task-oriented and women are more relationally oriented. Of course, men have relationships too, and women also have tasks, but their respective orientations to the world are different. The creation account bears this out. In the order of creation, the man is formed first. He is given a job before he is given a wife. The woman is created second. She is created to be his helper so he can fulfill his assigned tasks. Our natural proclivities fit these different roles. Men tend to be more analytical and objective, women more intuitive and empathetic. Men are leaders and initiators, while women are completers and glorifiers. She will finish what he starts. He kills an animal, she cooks it. He builds a house, she decorates it. And so on. There can be no denying that men and women see the world and act in the world differently.

But what happens when these differences lead to disagreements? How often do you hear about a husband and wife arguing over some aspect of how to raise their children? She sees the issue one way; he sees it another. Who's right? Who has the superior perspective? More often than not, both mom and dad are seeing important aspects of the situation, but both are also missing the whole. Only if they piece together their partial understandings will they arrive at a holistic view. Neither the masculine nor feminine view of the world is complete in itself; true wisdom is found when they are combined together into one. Children suffer a great deal when one spouse completely dominates the child-rearing paradigm in the home. A child's life is greatly enriched when his parents blend together their respective insights and perspectives.

Husbands and wives must learn to appreciate their differences in perspective, insofar as these stem from God-designed differences between the sexes. In fact, the book of Proverbs depicts the pursuit of wisdom as a kind of courtship between a man and a woman for just this reason. The son on the pathway to wisdom not only embraces the right woman (Lady Wisdom rather than Harlot Folly), but in doing so learns to value her way of seeing the world. This is why sons are commanded not only to obey their fathers, but to learn from their mothers as well (Prov. 1:8–9). At the end of Proverbs, we find the wise king reigning with his wise queen by his side as his trusted friend, confidant, and counselor (Prov. 30–31). This is exactly what the Christian marriage should look like. As two Christian spouses get to know one another deeply, they each learn to see the world the way the other sees it. Proverbs depicts growth in wisdom as the product of interfacing with the opposite gender in love and respect. The best way to grow in wisdom is listen to and learn from your spouse. Becoming wise means becoming a disciple of your spouse.

But, alas, this takes great effort and patience. If a man constantly interrupts his wife or simply refuses to listen to her, he's going to be an even bigger fool in the future than he is today. He must humble himself and come to appreciate her way of seeing things. A lot of men scoff at their wives' perspectives and fears. But he must treat her as his Lady Wisdom, his own personal tutor in prudence. Men, God did not give you a "feminine side," as you hear so often today; instead He has given you a wife. You need to get in touch with her if you want to be wise.

But this is not just a problem for male chauvinists. Frankly, in a culture overrun with egalitarianism and feminism, as our own is, all too many women dismiss the masculine perspective as brutish and silly. Women, this must not be; your husband has something vital to teach you about the world. As a woman gets to know her husband, she grows in wisdom. She must learn to seek and respect his point of view more than she does her mother's or her girlfriends'. A mature Christian marriage is one where a husband and wife never stop getting to know each other and where there is mutual appreciation for the perspective of each other. This is true wisdom and true maturity.

So we have seen how marriage helps us grow in forgiveness, humility, and wisdom. As a final example, consider how marriage teaches us about prayer. God uses marriage to stimulate us to prayer and teach us how prayer works. Peter says, "Likewise, husbands, live with your wives in an understanding way, showing honor to the woman as the weaker vessel, since they are heirs with you of the grace of life, so that your prayers may not be hindered" (1 Pet. 3:7).

God says to husbands, "If you do not listen to your wife, if you do not take her cares and concerns seriously, I will not take your cares and concerns seriously either." If you are a married man, you need to understand that God has put this condition on your prayer life. You must live with your wife in understanding, listening to her and serving her. Only then can you be confident that God will hear you and serve you by answering your prayers. God puts a kind of positive pressure on the prayer lives of Christian husbands by giving them this *lex talionis* principle. God tells men, 'How you treat your wife is how I will treat you." We might think the man with a great prayer life is going to have a great marriage, and that is no doubt true, but 1 Peter 3 pushes us in the opposite direction: having a great marriage is the key and impetus to a strong prayer life. If you want to have your prayers answered, be a good husband.

To conclude, we have seen three purposes God has built into marriage, all of which are under attack in our culture. First, marriage is for the sake of gospel symbolism. As husbands and wives fulfill their assigned roles, they image Christ and the Church to the world and thus "preach" the gospel. Second, marriage is for the sake of companionship. Husbands and wives befriend one another through thick and thin, and in this friendship encourage one another to keep walking with Christ as they journey together towards resurrection glory. And finally, marriage is a means of transformation and maturation. As spouses grow in their love and appreciation for one another, they learn how to practice Christian basics like forgiveness, humility, and prayer. But they also learn wisdom and thus become kings and queens over their God-given realms. The best defense of the biblical *doctrine* of marriage is the biblical *practice* of marriage. Marriage becomes its own best defense when we do married life God's way.

# Chapter 7
# The Blessed Family
*Rich Lusk*

¹ Blessed is every one who fears the LORD,
  Who walks in His ways.

² When you eat the labor of your hands,
    You shall be happy, and it shall be well with
      you.
³ Your wife shall be like a fruitful vine
    In the very heart of your house,
    Your children like olive plants
    All around your table.
⁴ Behold, thus shall the man be blessed
    Who fears the LORD.

⁵ The LORD bless you out of Zion,
    And may you see the good of Jerusalem
    All the days of your life.
⁶ Yes, may you see your children's children.

  Peace be upon Israel!

                                    Psalm 128

Psalm 128, along with its counterpart Psalm 127, is known as a "family psalm." It is full of both wisdom and beauty as it crystallizes the biblical vision of a household under the blessing of God. It might be easy to treat this psalm as a kind of verbal Norman Rockwell painting with the family feasting together around the dinner table with a huge turkey and all the trimmings right in the center. But actually if we unpack the imagery of this psalm as we should, we find there is nothing sentimental here. Indeed, the psalmist has provided us with a theologically rich and vibrantly practical model of family life that is uniquely biblical and covenantal in its origin, shape, and goal.

Before delving into this psalm, it is crucial for us to put the family in its proper context. Where does family fit into a biblical view of the world? How important is the family anyway? Is the family all it's cracked up to be by the "family values" folks? Is it possible to overemphasize the family in our day? And how do our families and homes relate to the family and household of God, the Church?

We must understand: *The one and only family that has ultimate significance is the family of God.* The church is not just a collection of families but is itself the family of God. Jesus makes it clear that His family, the Church, takes precedence over the biological family as well as over any kind of ethnic or national loyalty. Jesus calls His disciples away from their families, thus, relativizing the importance of the biological family even in the middle of a deeply patriarchal society. In Matthew 4, Jesus calls James and John to be His followers, and "immediately they left the boat *and their father* and followed Him" (Matt. 4:22). They not only left their nets (meaning their occupation as fishermen) behind to become apostles, but they left their father behind as well.

In following Jesus, they were becoming part of the new family He was forming around himself.

In Mark 3, Jesus is told that His family members are out looking for Him. Jesus says that whoever does the will of God (which means following Him) is "my brother and sister and mother" (Mark 3:31–34). Again, Jesus made it clear He was forming a new family, no longer defined in terms of kinship or blood, but rather in terms of loyalty to Him.

In Matthew 10, Jesus says He came to "set a man against his father, and a daughter against her mother, and a daughter-in-law against her mother-in-law. And a person's enemies will be those of his own household" (vv. 35–36). Jesus is announcing that the kingdom of God is breaking into history and ripping the old world apart. In light of the dawning of the kingdom of God, all other attachments and relationships are relativized. There is a new society, a new family being formed, and if necessary, you have to be willing to leave everything else behind for Jesus' sake in order to enter His kingdom.

Jesus severs the old ties; our hope is that He re-attaches them in a new way. To be sure, Jesus slays the ancient patriarchal family with its totalizing (and often tyrannizing) authority. But He also promises to renew family bonds so that spouses and parents and children can live harmoniously as fellow citizens in His kingdom. Thus, Jesus also sanctified marriage (Matt. 19:1–10) and blessed children (Matt. 19:13–14). In Jesus, husbandry and fatherhood can be restored to their original purpose and brought to perfection. The "anti-family" (or "family as rival to the kingdom") passages are important, but they do not tell the whole story by themselves. The kingdom not only challenges those who would idolize the family, but the kingdom redeems the family as well. Depending on our family situation, one side or the other may have more relevance for us. Jesus may stand for or against a family, depending on that family's stance towards His kingdom.

Certainly, the kingdom of God has ultimate primacy over everything. On the one hand, this means that even the natural family, which is obviously a God-created and ordained institution, becomes dispensable and disposable in light of the coming of the kingdom. If your family stands between you and Jesus, you must break ties with your family so you can adhere to Jesus. Just ask any Muslim convert to Christian faith how hard, but how necessary, this is! On the other hand, there are clearly ways in which Jesus is radically pro-family and desires to bring our families, in their entirety, into His kingdom to make them recipients of and agents of His grace. This doesn't always happen, but it is clearly held out as the ideal. Hence, the New Testament continues the Old Testament pattern of household salvation.

This overarching framework is the context within which we must give a Christian reading and application of Psalm 128. The Bible has a lot to say about the family, but all too often we have failed to notice how it puts the family in this broader context of the Kingdom of God. The Kingdom of God is ultimate; our families are penultimate. Our families are good, but they are not the greatest good. We should long for our families to be redeemed, whole and intact, but if that proves impossible, we should consider loyalty to Jesus and His family the higher priority.

When we turn our attention to places in the Scriptures that address the family in a positive way, what do we find? Psalm 128 is a psalm that celebrates the blessings of family life when the family is ordered as God designs and commands. God is for this family, and this family is for Him. This psalm sketches a picture of what family life looks like inside the kingdom of God. It is written from the perspective of the husband and father as the head of his household, responsible for its protection, provision, and well-being. As a result, I will primarily address my comments here to husbands and fathers. Men, listen up!

The psalmist begins: "Blessed is every one who fears the LORD, who walks in His ways!" This is a purposeful echo of the first psalm, which says, "Blessed is the man who walks not in the counsel of the wicked, nor stands in the way of sinners, nor sits in the seat of scoffers; but his delight is in the law of the LORD."

We see in Psalm 1 that the key to blessedness is doing life God's way. The blessed life is found in submitting yourself to God's pattern, living by faith according to God's design.

Psalm 128 may be viewed as a specific application of the principle of Psalm 1 to the realm of family life. This psalm shows us that the most important ingredient in a blessed family life is the faithfulness and godliness of the husband and father. If a man is not experiencing the blessing of God in his family life, it is not his wife's fault, nor is it the children's fault. It is the man's fault. The responsibility for securing God's blessing on the home rests on his shoulders. Every individual answers to God individually, but husbands and fathers also answer to God for their households as a whole.

Psalm 128 profiles the God-fearing family man. What does it mean to fear God? The book of Proverbs teaches us that the fear of the Lord is the beginning of wisdom.

Fearing God means seeing who God is and who you are in relation to Him. Fearing God leads to humility and maturity. The mature man knows how to manage his life according to God's Word; he humbles himself before God and insists God knows best. He doesn't seek the path of least resistance or of instant popularity; rather, he commits himself to obeying God because he knows he must ultimately answer to God not only for his own life, but for the state of his family.

Men have a widespread problem in our culture today. Boys are growing up physically but are failing to mature in other ways. They grow older without growing up. There has been a revolt against maturity among men in our culture, but in reality this is a revolt against the blessing of God. If you want God's blessing you must seek to walk in His commandments, fearing and trusting Him always. And incidentally, no Christian woman ever regretted marrying a God-fearing man and wished she had married someone who didn't fear God instead.

This is the kind of man for whom an unmarried Christian woman should look. A godly man measures his life's success in terms of obedience and faithfulness to God no matter what it costs him. The godly man knows that success in his workplace is not worth it if it comes at the price of domestic failure. He knows success in any other domain means nothing if he does not have the blessing of God resting on his family. He knows the most important thing in life is seeking and securing God's blessing. Psalm 128:1 teaches that being a good family man starts with being a good Christian.

What does the blessed man look like in familial relationships? In verse 3, the psalmist declares, "Your wife will

be like a fruitful vine within your house; your children will
be like olive shoots around your table." The man may be the
head, but she is the heart. A wife does not simply *make* the
home; in a deep way, she *is* the home. She is the glory and
heartbeat of the home. She is described here as a fruitful
vine. What does it mean for her to be a vine? Vines produce
grapes from which we get wine. This is a fitting picture of
the godly woman who brings joy to her husband, even as
wine makes the heart glad. The godly husband delights in
his wife and she feels his pleasure as she plays her role in the
home. As she wraps her love around the home, enclosing
it within herself, she fills it with joy and life. While the man
is "in charge" of his family, his wife will actually do much
more on a day-to-day basis to shape the environment and
ethos of the home.

What makes her a *fruitful* vine? She is well taken care
of; vines do not bear fruit unless they are nurtured. Paul
unpacks this in Ephesians 5 when he commands husbands
to nourish and cherish their wives the way Jesus does the
Church. Men, the meaning of this is plain: *Your wife should
feel like she is married to Jesus.* That is the standard and goal for
the godly man. Men, you must treat your wives the way Jesus
treats the Church. Ask yourself: "How much grace, mercy,
patience, and encouragement does Jesus offer His Bride?
To what lengths was He willing to go to demonstrate His
love for her? How much does He forgive her and care for
her? Does He love her with a cheap love or a costly love?"

Men, you must take Jesus as your model for husbandry.
Does Jesus say to His Church, "I will only love you if you
first meet my demands and expectations?" No. Jesus always
takes loving initiative with His bride. He does not say to
His bride, "I will do my part if and only if you do yours."

No, Jesus does not demand change and growth as a condition of being loved; rather, His love empowers growth and change in His bride. Does Jesus exalt himself over her and boss His bride around? No. Jesus came to deny himself. He came not to be served by the bride, but to serve her. Jesus comes with a service mindset in relation to His bride. How does Jesus deal with the fears and concerns of His bride? He does not mock her fears or exploit her insecurities. He shows her compassion and love, even when she is weak. Men, you must do the same. Husbands, do not take advantage of your wife's inclination to serve, as many men do. Make it your aim to give to your wife, and you will find she outpaces your giving every time. I have never known a man who was able to out-give his wife, but if a man tries to do so, he is sure to have a very happy and blessed marriage!

Husbands, your wife will be a fruitful vine when you are laying your life down for her again and again, when you are nurturing her with your love and gentleness. Jesus-like love brings a woman security and joy. It calms her anxieties and gives her confidence. Men, the measure of your love for your wife must be Jesus' love for His bride. Don't settle for comparing yourself to a lesser standard; to do so is to sell yourself, and especially your wife, short. Rather, learn to die to your own agenda and become a servant in your home. Of course, this kind of sacrificial, self-giving love is just a special application of the kind of glad obedience and service every Christian should render, whatever his or her God-appointed role and station in life. Again, we see *the key to being a good husband is simply being a good Christian.*

Frankly, a lot of men are knuckleheads when it comes to loving their wives. Men, you need to understand the burdens your wife is bearing. If your wife is raising small children, she has perhaps the most demanding and difficult job in the world. A bad day at the office is no match for a bad day at home. Your wife is carrying on a vital ministry to your children and she needs your support. In Matthew 25:31–46, Jesus says at the last day He will praise His faithful servants who have fed the hungry, clothed the naked, and cared for the sick because these deeds, done for the least of these, are done to and for Jesus Himself. Well, guess what, men, your wives are carrying on Matthew 25 ministries all day long, day after day. Our wives are feeding hungry kids, clothing naked kids, and caring for sick kids all day long, day after day, week after week, month after month, year after year. Jesus will praise her for it; she is doing a good work in His eyes. Husbands, you need to validate her, honor her, and praise her as well. If Jesus will praise her at the last day, you have to praise her *right now*.

Remember that if your wife is raising kids at home, she is doing something politically incorrect and radically counter-cultural in our day. She will not be receiving any support from the world around her. Thus, she needs the support and encouragement and help of her husband. She needs to know you value her labors.

I heard an interesting story a while back. A pastor once invited people who were struggling with anger problems to meet with him after the worship service. Nineteen people showed up . . . and every single one was a mother with young children in the home! My guess is that these moms were really not less sanctified than the rest of the congregation. They just had a harder job that was pushing them past the breaking point. These moms were struggling with anger because they were not being tended to and cultivated the way they should have been. Maybe if their husbands were more patient and helpful, these moms would not have been on edge as often. Men, the point is this: in any ordinary set of circumstances, if your wife is not flourishing and fruitful, you are the one with a problem. Don't try to "fix" her; fix yourself, and she'll begin to bear abundant fruit again.

What about the blessed man and his children? What is the blessed man like as a father? The psalmist says that "your sons will be like olive plants around your table."

What does it mean for our children to be little olives? The olive plant is very significant in Scriptures. In Genesis 8, as the flood waters are receding, Noah sends out a dove. The dove returns with an olive branch as the waters begin to part and the dry land re-emerges. Thus, the olive becomes a symbol of the new creation. The olive means God's warfare against humanity is over and peace now reigns. Later in Scripture, we find the cherubim on the Ark of the Covenant in the Most Holy Place in the temple were carved from olive wood (1 Kgs. 6:23). A holy place calls for holy wood and so olive wood is used.

But there are additional layers to this olive symbolism. Olive oil, the oil flowing through the plant, is presented as a symbol of the Spirit and is used in the anointing of priests and kings. Judges 9:9 suggests that olives are the rightful kings of the plant world. Jesus gives a crucial prophetic discourse on the Mount of Olives (Matt. 24). The great events of the gospel took place on or in the immediate vicinity of the Mount of Olives, and thus in a grove of olive trees: Jesus' suffering in Gethsemane (which means "olive press"), betrayal, arrest, crucifixion, resurrection, and ascension all occur in an Olivet environment. Jesus was likely crucified on an olive tree, given that Golgotha was located on the Mount of Olives.[1] This is because the place of the cross is the new altar and must correspond to the Most Holy Place. Jesus also ascended from earth up into heaven from the Mount of Olives. Olive trees are symbolic connection points with the celestial realm. Jesus is the ultimate Olive Tree.

But, of course, this means His Church must be signified by olives as well. In Romans 11, the olive tree is used to symbolize God's holy people, Israel, in both old covenant and new covenant forms. Natural branches from the olive tree (the Jews) may be broken out because of unbelief, while wild olive branches (Gentiles) may be grafted in by faith, but either way the olive plant clearly symbolizes the covenant community. The patriarchs are olive roots; we are olive branches.

All of this taken together is very suggestive. The olive plant is clearly the holiest plant in the Bible's symbolic economy. There are priestly, kingly, messianic, new creation, and heavenly associations, not to mention connections with the cross and the Spirit. The multi-layered symbolism of the olive contains virtually every element of the gospel. What the psalmist is saying about the status of our children, then, should be clear. The children of the blessed man are holy. They belong to God and are loved by God. They are part of His people and His new creation. They are kings and priests with us. They have the oil of the Spirit flowing within them. They share in Christ's sacrifice and are called to live sacrificially. They are part of the church community but must persevere in faith and repentance.

---

[1] Cf. James B. Jordan, "Christ in the Holy of Holies: The Meaning of the Mount of Olives," *Biblical Horizons* 84 (April 1996). Online: http://www.biblicalhorizons.com/biblical-horizons/no-84-christ-in-the-holy-of-holies-the-meaning-of-the-mount-of-olives/.

These truths about the status and identity of our children before God serve as the foundation for everything else the Bible has to say about parenting. Fathers, you must recognize these truths about your children. You must count and treat your children as members of the people of God from infancy onwards, until and unless they prove otherwise. They are saints because God makes them saints. We do not wait for them to grow up and choose to become olive branches. Rather, God declares and promises to us that they are already little olive plants even in their youth. Our children are not noxious weeds; they are olive plants in God's field, and must be raised accordingly so they will be strong and fruitful olive trees when fully grown.

Of course, I don't have to tell you this is deeply counter-cultural even in the Church. Some parents feel it is completely within their rights to impose piano lessons and swimming practices on their children. But when it comes to religious things, they say they want their children to "make their own decision." But God tells parents they must impose a religious identity on their children—a specifically Christian religious identity. God says our children are His. He has claimed them from the beginning. We are to raise them up in His way. Beginning with baptism, we are to give our children to God and claim the promises He makes to and about them.

The United Nations adopted a children's rights declaration a few years ago called the "Convention on the Rights of the Child." Every member nation, except the United States and Somalia (an odd pair, to say the least!), accepted the document. Included in the document's list of every child's rights is the right of the child to make his own decision about religion. Think about the astounding implications of that for Christian parents! This UN document, ratified by nearly two hundred nations in the world, essentially makes infant baptism an international crime. Why? Because children baptized in infancy have a Christian identity imposed on them from the earliest days of their lives. The document contradicts the practice of infant baptism because baptized children are made Christians before they can openly and independently consent.[2]

The document is well intentioned and, no doubt, does many good things to curb global abuse of children, but it is not acceptable to any covenantal Christian who wants to raise his children up in the way of the Lord. What the world calls indoctrination and brainwashing, Paul calls raising our children in the nurture and admonition of the Lord. We do not wait for our children to get older and then hope they choose the Lord; instead, we tell them from their earliest days that God has already chosen them and appointed them to bear much fruit. We know that our children can never be religiously neutral, but God has graciously promised to include them in His covenant. He is our God and the God of our children. Lord willing, they will grow up never remembering a day when they did not know, trust, and love their Heavenly Father.

The blessed man will not accept what the world says about his children. He will believe what God says about his children. God says they are olive plants, holy and beloved. Thus, the godly man will water his children in baptism and fertilize them with the Scriptures and the Lord's Supper so they can bring forth juicy olives, full of the oil of the Spirit. We are called to believe this about our children. Our children are not weeds in need of uprooting, but olive plants

---

[2] The document also seeks to outlaw corporal punishment, but that is a matter we will not take up here.

in need of nurturing and watering so they will bring forth Spiritual fruit. The blessed man knows the starting point of all faithful parenting is receiving our children as olive plants and believing what God says about them. Godly fathering flows from faith in God's promises, which means (once again) *the key to being a good dad is being a good Christian.*

The imagery of Psalm 128:3 meshes well with the teaching of Jesus. In Matthew 18:5 Jesus says, "Whoever receives one such child in my name receives me." What does it mean to receive a child in Jesus' name? It means to receive him as one who bears the name of Jesus, not because of anything in the child by nature, but because the child is graciously included in God's covenant. Note that Jesus used similar language for His apostles in Matthew 10, when He said, "He who receives you, receives me." The apostles carry the presence of Jesus with them. They are in union with Jesus and represent Him so that those who receive them actually receive Jesus. But now we find the same is true for covenant children: receiving them in Jesus' name is a way of receiving Jesus himself. It is as though when God gives us children, He is sending us apostles of Jesus! Will we receive them as apostles, as dignitaries and ambassadors of Jesus' kingdom? Or will we say, "No, you're too young to represent Jesus"? The blessed man of Psalm 128 knows his children are holy and filled with the Spirit. He knows his job is to cultivate the grace given to his children so they will grow in grace and not become covenant breakers.

On the surface, Psalm 128 does not seem to give us any tips or techniques for parenting. It does not say anything explicit about discipline, education, or other matters that dominate most of our books on parenting. There is really only one thing that Psalm 128 teaches us about parenting:

*the spiritual identity of our children.* But this turns out to be the most practical thing we can know about our children! Our children are olive plants; like every other member of the people of God, they are to be treated and counted as fellow kingdom citizens and fellow-heirs of the grace of eternal life. Following how-to formulas will not get you the child-rearing results you desire apart from trusting God's promises and declarations about your children. By starting with what God says, we are set free to do what God says to do *by faith.* If we believe the promises of God about our children, then we will learn to love, discipline, teach, and nurture them *by faith.* Blessed parenting is *by faith* from beginning to end.

Finally, if there is a tip or technique for parents in Psalm 128, it's this: The blessed family eats together. They feast and converse together around the table. Just as the table is central in the Church, so it is central in the family. The blessed man will teach his olive plants how to participate in the family meal with courtesy, respect for others, self-discipline, service, and love. The culture of the table becomes the culture of the home, which in turn becomes the culture of the family's life in all they do. Culture always flows downstream from the table; the godly man will remember that and plan his mealtimes accordingly.

There is obviously much more that could be said about the godly family and the godly family man from Psalm 128 (not to mention its companion piece, Psalm 127). But hopefully these remarks are sufficient to give a thumbnail sketch of what covenant parenting should look like "on the ground," which is where it counts. For the blessed man knows mere knowledge is not enough; he must lead his family by putting into practice all he has learned from the Word of God. Get to work, men!